GALATIANS
The Charter of Christian Liberty

GALATIANS:
The Charter of Christian Liberty

by

MERRILL C. TENNEY

DEAN OF THE GRADUATE SCHOOL,
WHEATON COLLEGE, WHEATON, ILLINOIS

REVISED AND ENLARGED EDITION

WM. B. EERDMANS PUBLISHING CO.
GRAND RAPIDS   MICHIGAN

PHOTOLITHOPRINTED BY EERDMANS PRINTING COMPANY
GRAND RAPIDS, MICHIGAN, UNITED STATES OF AMERICA

In memory of

MY MOTHER

*who first taught me
to study
the Word of God*

PREFACE

For some time the author has had the conviction that there is room in the field of Biblical exegesis for a work which should encourage the lover of the Bible to pursue its study for himself. There are so many treasures in the Word of God that no one commentary or treatise can contain all of them; and since one book can deal with only a few at the most, the best procedure is to show how the treasures can be unlocked, and then to let the reader use the key for himself.

Many extensive commentaries and critical essays have been written on Galatians, and this book does not pretend to supersede them. It is an attempt to present ten different approaches to the meaning of the Biblical text, and to illustrate each so that the reader can imitate the procedure and thus have the joy of making original discoveries in the divine revelation. The sum total of these illustrations will provide a representative treatment of Galatians.

The writer acknowledges gratefully the wise editorial counsel and unstinted aid of his wife, Helen J. Tenney. Thanks are due also to Dr. V. R. Edman, President of Wheaton College, who read the first draft and who suggested many improvements, and to Miss Edna Smallwood, who assisted in copying the text. To these, and to the many unnamed friends who have contributed unconsciously to the content of this book, it is offered as a tribute of gratitude.   M.C.T.

PREFACE TO THE REVISED EDITION

The wide use of this book as a classroom text and as a guide to general Bible study has prompted this revision. Its chief feature is the addition of one chapter on the comparative method of Bible study, which should increase its value in the interpretation of Galatians, and which should make it a greater help in the general understanding of Scripture.

A few small corrections have been made elsewhere in the text, and in the bibliography to bring it up to date. This new volume is offered to the public in the hope that its usefulness will be multiplied.

M.C.T.

CONTENTS

LIST OF CHARTS AND DIAGRAMS

INTRODUCTION

The Book of Galatians

INTRODUCTION

THE BOOK OF GALATIANS

Importance of the Book

The book of Galatians is one of the shorter epistles of Paul. In any Bible of ordinary size it occupies not more than eight pages of two columns each, and it can be read carefully though rapidly in twenty minutes. As a piece of literature it is not remarkable for artistry or beauty; nor would a casual reader be likely to read it twice for the sheer aesthetic delight of doing so. Its historic allusions are obscure, and the arguments do not appear to be relevant to modern issues. In the vast collection of the writings of antiquity it seems to be inconspicuous and unimportant when compared to the dramas of Euripides or to the historical writings of Tacitus.

Few books, however, have had a more profound influence on the history of mankind than has this small tract, for such it could be called. Christianity might have been just one more Jewish sect, and the thought of the Western world might have been entirely pagan had it never been written. Galatians embodies the germinal teaching on Christian freedom which separated Christianity from Judaism, and which launched it upon a career of missionary conquest. It was the cornerstone of the Protestant Reformation, because its teaching of salvation by grace alone became the dominant theme of the preaching of the Reformers. Luther's *Commentary on Galatians* was the reasoned manifesto of the revolt against the Roman ritual and hierarchy, which, more than any other single document, revived the knowledge of Biblical truth in the minds of the people. It has been called "the Magna Charta of spiritual emancipation," [1] for on its principles is formed the whole faith of a free church.

In more recent times, Galatians has played an important part in the study of the Scriptures. When the modern critical approach to the Bible was initiated at the turn of the nineteenth century, this book was recognized as a primary document in the discussion of all matters pertaining to the history of the Christian movement. F. C. Baur, founder of the Tubingen school of criticism which opened the rationalistic attack on the orthodox attitude to the New Testament, promulgated the theory that its writings were the surviving echoes of partisan strife between Judaistic and Gentile Christians as championed respectively by Peter and Paul. He discarded some of them as not written by the authors to which they were traditionally attributed, and rejected the authority of Acts on the ground that it was a late attempt to smooth over the evidences of disagreement so that the unity of the church might be preserved. He did concede that Galatians was genuinely Pauline. [2] He, and most of those who followed him, regarded its statements as written by a contemporary of the events described, and as giving a reliable, though perhaps fragmentary, account of the controversies and growth of primitive Christianity. When almost everything else in the early tradition was questioned, Galatians was still recognized as a sound basis for historical interpretation. "Here at least," says E. F. Scott, "there is firm ground on which the historian can proceed to build." [3]

---

1. F. W. Farrar, *Messages of the Books of the Bible,* (London: Macmillan & Co., Ltd., 1909) I, 258.

2. Theodor Zahn, *Introduction to the New Testament,* (translated from the third German edition; New York: Charles Scribner's Sons, 1909), I, 154.

3. E. F. Scott, *The Literature of the New Testament,* (New York: Columbia University Press, 1932), p. 145.

There are many aspects of early Christianity that may never be fully known because pertinent information is lacking. The church of the apostolic age was more concerned with making history than it was with writing history. Such information as exists in Galatians is accurate, and is adequate to afford a firm foundation for thinking. Like a candle in a cave, it may not illumine every remote corner, but it gives sufficient light so that one may make his way confidently through the darkness. It does not resolve all historical puzzles, but it does answer definitely the main question: What was the prime contribution of apostolic Christianity to human need?

The prominence of Galatians in historical criticism is great only because of its transcendent importance to Christian theology. Even though most of its teaching was repeated in other epistles of Paul, in none of them is the central principle of saving faith in Christ stated as cogently and as concisely as it is here. The key verse, Galatians 2:20, "I have been crucified with Christ; and it is no longer I that live, but Christ liveth in me: and that *life* which I now live in the flesh I live in faith, *the faith* which is in the Son of God, who loved me and gave himself up for me," unites the objective theological concept of the book with the subjective personal experience of the author. The essence of theoretical Christianity is thus united with its practical expression in one significant sentence, of which Galatians is an expanded interpretation.

Objectively, Galatians asserts that salvation is freely bestowed by God in response to faith which is founded upon His personal revelation through His gospel. Paul himself said of that gospel, "Neither did I receive it from man, nor was I taught it, but *it came to me* through revelation of Jesus Christ" (1:12). If the message is a revelation from God, it is not a human device, but is the divine disclosure of eternal truth. Truth, then, is both man's freedom and man's limitation. It is his freedom because it saves him from superstition, ignorance, and degradation; it is his limitation because it demands of him a hearing, and he neglects it to his own peril. Christian liberty originates in the revelation of God which defines human weakness and which makes available God's saving power. In this truth man finds his true liberty, for liberty consists not in the ability to disobey God with impunity, but in the ability to obey Him spontaneously without effective hindrance. The power of God as revealed in "the Son of God who loved me and gave himself up for me" is the sure antidote for the enslavement of the human spirit.

Subjectively, the inner life of the Christian is discussed here in its relation to God. The destruction of sin, the creation of a new man, the exercise of faith, and the enjoyment of consequent liberty are all presented in the natural setting of actual experience, illustrated by biographical allusions. This book is a series of pictures of what spiritual life should be, not just a formulary of precepts. The writer was describing what he himself was enjoying after having lived a large part of his life in legalistic bondage. The use of the first person singular in Galatians 2:20 is no mere editorial device, but is the expression of personal feeling which burst the bounds of literary restraint. Paul could not contain himself as he contemplated the possibility that the spontaneous spiritual life of the Galatian Christians might be stifled by the unnecessary imposition upon them of arguments and ceremonies which were irrelevant to salvation. Inner fruitfulness of the spirit is more important than outward conformity of the flesh; and if the Holy Spirit is dominant within, the action of the outward man will be governed accordingly. "Christ liveth in me" is the subjective aspect of liberty, because the Christian life is thus not a struggle between the reluctant will of man and the domineering will of God, but becomes the constant control of the inner life by Christ. His will becomes regnant by free accord, not by repressive compulsion.

From this experience which he had undergone himself, Paul wrote to the Galatians that they might not be cheated of the freedom which was theirs by right. The truth he expounded so vigorously and so ably is still of the utmost value to those who think of the Christian life as a succession of inhibitions rather than as a continual expression of divine victories.

Objectively and subjectively, then, Galatians is the charter of freedom from externalism in worship and from frustration in personal spiritual life. As the Lord Jesus Himself said: "If ye abide in my word [faith in the revelation],*then* are ye truly my disciples; and ye shall know [experience] the truth [objective theology], and the truth shall make you free [subjective experience]" (John 8:31, 32).

History of the Study of Galatians

The book of Galatians has been used in the church almost continuously since the day it was written. It is possible that Romans was Paul's own expansion of it; for the two epistles are quite similar in theme and content. Romans treats the subject of salvation by faith much more systematically and extensively than does Galatians. Although the priority of the latter cannot be established with absolute finality because of the uncertainty of its date, the broader and less polemic tone of Romans seemingly indicates that it was written when controversy had abated and when the church at large needed counsel in its thinking more than reproof for its errors.

In the subapostolic era Polycarp evidently alluded at least twice to Galatians in his *Epistle to the Philippians,* for he says "God is not mocked," which accords exactly with Galatians 6:7, and also says that God "raised him [Christ] from the dead," which is possibly from Galatians 1:1. [4] The references to Galatians in the writings of Ignatius are not sufficiently clear to warrant comment. Those that are identifiable occur in the longer version of Ignatius' works which most scholars

---

4. *Epistle of Polycarp to the Philippians,* V, XII.

regard as spurious. They would, therefore, have no value as criteria of the use of Galatians in the subapostolic age. [5]

In the second century Galatians was widely recognized and used. No less than twenty-five verses were quoted from it by Irenaeus [6] who mentioned the epistle by name. [7] It was treated in the commentaries of Origen, which were written about A.D. 200, and from that time on it was frequently discussed in the literature both of the Eastern and Western churches. Jerome and Pelagius in the fourth century, and a group of Latin writers in the ninth century made it the subject of their studies. From 900 to 1500 few commentaries of any kind were written. In the sixteenth century, during the Reformation, interest in Bible study revived; and, through the commentary of Luther, Galatians came into prominence once again in the literature of the church.

In the modern era Galatians has received a fair share of the attention of exegetes and critics. For an extensive list of works relating to it the reader should consult the bibliography at the end of this volume. In the late nineteenth century J. B. Lightfoot published his commentary, *St. Paul's Epistle to the Galatians,* which has been standard for more than half a century. Sir William Ramsay's *Historical Commentary on St. Paul's Epistle to the Galatians* supplemented Lightfoot's work by furnishing the historical and archaeological background of the epistle, whereas Lightfoot had devoted himself chiefly to an exegetical treatment of the text. The most recent thorough study is the *Critical and Exegetical Commentary on the Epistle to the Galatians* by Ernest De Witt Burton, which was published in 1920 in the series of the *International Critical Commentary.* The value of this last work is greatly enhanced by

5. See Epistles of Ignatius
   To the Romans VIII (Longer Version) — Galatians 2:20
   To the Philadelphians IV (Longer Version) — Galatians 3:28
6. By count of index in A. Roberts and J. Donaldson, *The Ante-Nicene Fathers* (Grand Rapids: Wm. B. Eerdmans Publishing Co., 1950), I, 601.
7. See Irenaeus *Against Heresies*, V, 11, 1.

the word studies and special notes which it contains. It is obvious that the book of Galatians has proved to be of perennial interest from the historical, critical, and theological standpoints.

Methods of Study

In order that the reader may profit most fully from Galatians, the study of the book is undertaken by ten different methods. *The Synthetic Method* approaches the book as a unit and seeks to understand its meaning as a whole. The method does not concern itself with detail, but with the broad outline of argument and of general application. *The Critical Method* examines carefully the statements and implications of the book in order to ascertain its reliability and its relation to the day and conditions in which it was professedly written. *The Biographical Method* reconstructs from such hints or statements as the book itself may supply the picture of the author and of his associates, and interprets their context in the light of their personalities. *The Historical Method* reproduces the historical and geographical setting of the book, and attempts to show how these affect its interpretation. *The Theological Method* codifies the teaching of the book according to the various doctrines with which it deals, and explains its spiritual emphases. *The Rhetorical Method* indicates how the use of syntax and figures of speech are employed to convey the doctrinal teaching, and defines the rules of interpretation as they relate to language. *The Topical Method* extracts from the text all references to a given topic, and translates their context into unified teaching on that one theme, such as *liberty,* or *sonship.* *The Analytical Method,* which is the opposite of *The Synthetic Method,* involves a detailed examination of the text or of some one portion of it, by analyzing its grammatical structure, and by the formulation of a detailed outline which will express exactly the meaning of that structure. *The Comparative Method* illumines the text by comparing or contrasting with the text related passages of Scripture. *The Devotional Method* seeks to apply the meaning of the language to the personal life of the reader.

Any one of these methods will produce good results in the understanding of Galatians, or of any other book of the Bible, but a combination of all of them is best for full comprehension of Scriptural truth. In the following pages the advantages and limitations of each one of these methods will be discussed and illustrated. Both the brevity and the importance of this epistle make it peculiarly suitable as an illustration of these methods of study, since the manner of approach and the fruitfulness of the result can be demonstrated in short compass

THE BOOK AS A WHOLE

THE SYNTHETIC METHOD

CHAPTER I

THE BOOK AS A WHOLE

The Synthetic Method

IN ORDER to appreciate the argument of Galatians, the book must first be read as a whole. None of the letters of Paul, nor any other single document of the New Testament for that matter, was divided originally into the chapters and verses that appear in modern Bibles. While there were undoubtedly divisions or stops of thought marked by transitions or by definite declarations of change of topic, each letter was intended to be read as a continuous whole, as letters are read now. Piecemeal perusal may yield gems of thought with each section, but the entire setting will be missed if each document is not treated as a unitary composition, framed to convey one main theme. Galatians is no exception to this rule, and it should be read as a unit if its real meaning is to be apprehended.

Definition of Method

The initial approach to the study of Galatians should therefore follow the simple method of reading through the book as a whole several times. The readings need not follow each other in immediate succession, but each reading should seek to deal with some different aspect of the total organization and teaching of the book, and at the end of that reading the results should be committed to paper. The thoughts stimulated by these repeated readings will give a fairly correct perspective of the actual content of the book when they have been collected and integrated.

The interpretation of a book in its totality by such a process of repeated reading and final integration of results is

called *the synthetic method.* The word *synthetic* is derived
from the Greek preposition *syn,* which means *together,* and
the verbal root *the,* which means *to put,* so that the resultant
meaning is "a putting together." Synthetic is the opposite of
analytic, which means "a taking apart." The synthetic method
ignores detail, and treats only of the interpretation of a document as a whole.

The First Reading: The Main Theme

The first reading of the book should be careful but rapid;
and the main quest should be for the central theme. What
idea is uppermost in the mind of the author, and how is he
seeking to develop it? Does any one verse or passage state
this idea more definitely than any other?

In Galatians such a passage occurs in 5:1:

> *For freedom did Christ set us free: stand fast there-
> fore, and be not entangled again in a yoke of bondage.*

Christian liberty is the central theme of the letter, particular-
ly as related to the believer's freedom from the bondage of legalism which is the natural consequence of attempting to earn
salvation by works. If man can obtain the favor of God by
his voluntary fulfillment of the ceremonial law, then his salvation depends upon the completeness of his obedience. Any de-
viation from the law exposes him to punishment and jeopard-
izes his salvation. Each small volition of life, therefore, must
be scrutinized carefully to ascertain whether it is in keeping
with the law of God, or whether it will transgress some expressed divine command and so bring the doer's destiny into
peril. Such a legalistic attitude produces spiritual bondage because the person involved becomes so engrossed with attend-
ing to the letter of the law that he overlooks its spirit. In
the words of the Saviour, he "strains out the gnat and swal-
lows the camel" (Matt. 23:24). Galatians seeks to show that

the believer is to be saved by faith in what Christ has done for him rather than by his own diligence in keeping the precepts of the revealed law.

The Second Reading: The Development

A second reading with the central theme in mind will show that this concept of freedom from the law is emphasized throughout the entire book. Paul declared boldly that "a man is not justified by the works of the law but through faith in Jesus Christ . . . because by the works of the law shall no flesh be justified" (2:16). He affirmed that "as many as are of the works of the law are under a curse" (3:10). The law is only "our tutor *to bring us* unto Christ, that we might be justified by faith" (3:24), and now that faith is come, we are no longer under a tutor, but have received "the adoption of sons" (4:5). The ceremony of the law, he said, is a dead letter, "for neither is circumcision anything, nor uncircumcision, but a new creature" (6:15).

The tone of the book is polemic. The reasoning is that of a man engaged in debate. The interrogations, posed in rapid succession (3:1-4), the frequent appeals to the individual reader (1:6, 10; 3:1, 2, 3, 4, 5, 15; 4:6, 13, 15, 16, 21; 5:1, 2, 13; 6:1, 10, 11, 17), the occasional expressions of exasperation (1:6-9; 2:4-6, 11; 3:1; 4:11; 5:2, 12, 21; 6:12), the tenseness of the logical argument (chapter 3) all show that this epistle is controversial in its nature. It is not an essay, written merely to entertain or to instruct complacent believers. It was written to stimulate theological thought and to rouse an endangered church to action. Its words are sharp as the edge of a dagger, and its thought savors of battle smoke.

Two general problems appear in Galatians: the problem of a salvation of the soul by works versus a salvation by faith; and the problem of a perfection by works rather than a perfection by faith. The former is peculiarly the problem of the unsaved formalist whose religion consists chiefly in a negative attitude toward life expressed by prohibitions. Parallel to this problem and a logical counterpart to it is the problem of the believer who desires to be perfected in his moral and spiritual nature, and who relies upon the law for that perfection (3:3). Both of these problems may be subsumed under the one head of legalism for they are essentially the one question related to two spheres of life. [1] They need not be treated as representative of two different parties within the Galatian churches, but rather they indicate the two natural consequences of legalism in any body of Christians.

The second of these problems is quite as much the result of ignorance as of wilful disobedience; in fact, it is often the outcome of a desire to attain a higher degree of spirituality than the level with which the average believer is content. As soon as the believer comprehends the possibilities that salvation presents to the development of the inner life, he desires to go on to the perfection of accomplishment and of character. He does not, however, always realize the best method of achieving this end. Because he feels that redemption has freed him from the penalties of the law, he may take for granted that he is also released from the law's standards of holiness, and so he may assume the attitude that "I am saved by grace, and may now do as I please." On the other hand, he may, because of his experience of salvation, feel all the more obligated to keep the precepts of God, and he may fall into bondage to the restraints expressed in the law. He will seek to

---

1. For a novel presentation of these two viewpoints, see James H. Ropes' *The Singular Problem of the Epistle to the Galatians*, (Cambridge: Harvard University Press, 1929), which is based on an earlier work by Lutgert. Ropes contends that there were two parties in the Galatian churches, the Judaizing party that sought to bring Gentile believers under the yoke of Judaism, and the "radicals" who repudiated Paul, and rejected the Old Testament completely, as Paul did not do (p. 10). Although it is altogether possible that there were radicals who carried Paul's attitude farther than he would have done, Ropes' argument for the existence of two utterly divergent parties seems to be strained.

achieve holiness by striving to keep all of the regulations and precepts of the law, and so will fall into the delusion that perfection can be earned.

Galatians is directed against both of these errors, though in its exposition the second has generally received less attention. Paul attacks it boldly, "Are ye so foolish? having begun in the Spirit, are ye now perfected in the flesh?" (3:3). He contends that the Spirit, not the letter; growth, not observance of ritual; fruitage, not negative restraint are the true marks of progress toward spiritual perfection.

The Third and Fourth Readings: Outline

The third and fourth readings of the book should produce a textual outline. The third reading should be exploratory. If the main theme is clearly in the mind of the reader, he should look for its logical development in the text before him. If the author was capable of writing a convincing work, he must have followed some plan. Whèther his plan will coincide exactly with the reader's idea of how the theme should be developed is not of supreme importance. The reader should prepare his mind to discover the author's logic and to follow it through by the latter's plan.

There are several possible ways of finding clues to the author's method. First, look for any announcement which the author himself may make concerning the content of his work. For instance, in I Corinthians Paul gives the main outline of that variegated epistle by specifying clearly the subjects to be discussed: "Now concerning the things whereof ye wrote . . ." (7:1), "Now concerning virgins . . ." (7:25), "Now concerning things sacrificed to idols . . ." (8:1). The turning points of the epistle can easily be established by the plain declarations of subject matter as stated.

Sometimes repeated phrases which are not open declarations of change of subject will afford an insight into the structure of a work. In the book of Hebrews the phrase "Let us," which

represents the hortatory subjunctive in Greek, may indicate the
exhortation which completes a section of teaching (Heb. 4:14,
16; 6:1; 10:22; 12:28; 13:13). The phrase, "When Jesus had
finished . . .," which recurs five times in the Gospel of Matthew
(7:28, 11:1, 13:53, 19:1, 26:1) marks five different stages
in the topical presentation of Jesus' career. One should not
conclude that the recurrences of a phrase are necessarily in-
dicative of the author's sequence of thought, for they may be
purely accidental and bear no relation to the structure at all.
On the other hand, when the author is not present to explain
what he had in mind, one must make use of every possible factor that can lead to the unraveling of the meaning of his writings.

When chronological, geographical, historical, and literary
divisions within some document coincide, the coincidences are
usually to be regarded as marking main divisions in the author's thought. [2]

In the absence of any stated or manifest clues such as those
mentioned above, abrupt changes of subject, or of person, or
of rhetorical form, such as a shift from narration to question-
ing or exhortation, will show that the author has launched upon a new subject and that recognition of the change should be
made in the outline.

The best way of identifying such changes is to follow the
text by paragraphs, to note the content of each paragraph as
a unit, and then to correlate the major changes discovered in
this process with the possible development of the main theme.
The results achieved by so doing will probably approximate
the original design of the author. Paragraphing, of course,
was not original, and represents only the judgment of the edi-
tors who set up the text as it now exists. It will, nevertheless,
supply a relatively sound basis for all ordinary study.

---

2. For illustration of this phenomenon in the Gospel of John, see the
author's work on *John: The Gospel of Belief* (Grand Rapids, Mich.: Wm.
B. Eerdmans Pub. Co., 1953), pp. 40, 41.

The subjoined chart presents the text of Galatians as divided into paragraphs both in the American Standard Version of the English Bible, [3] and in Eberhard Nestle's edition of the Greek text. [4] The general content of each paragraph is summarized in order that the sequence of thought may be followed.

At only two points do the paragraph divisions of the English and Greek texts occur at different places. English paragraph no. 2 ends with 1:10; Greek paragraph no. 2 ends with 1:9. The confusion is pardonable; for 1:10 may be taken either as explanatory of the sweeping imprecation in the preceding verses, or as introductory to the statement of independence which follows. The Greek paragraphing is preferable, for the anathema of verse 9 closes the statement of the problem which the occasion of the letter had posed, and verse 10 begins the personal defense which is the opening attack upon the problem of which the book treats.

The second variation occurs in Greek paragraph no. 4, which comprises the English paragraphs 7, 8, 9, and 10, ending at 4:7 with the words, "then an heir through God." From the end of English paragraph no. 10 there is complete agreement until the beginning of paragraph no. 16, where Greek paragraph no. 10 includes the English paragraphs no. 16 through no. 20. The English scheme makes the details of the argument easier to follow, since the paragraphing is broken down into smaller units.

The Greek paragraphing condenses the text into a smaller number of larger sections, and makes more apparent the broad divisions of the text.

---

3. The Holy Bible, containing the Old and New Testaments translated out of the original tongues, being the version set forth A. D. 1611 compared with the most ancient authorities and revised A. D. 1881-1885. Newly edited by the American Revision Committee A. D. 1901. Standard Edition. New York: Thomas Nelson & Sons, 1901.
4. NOVUM TESTAMENTUM GRAECE cum apparatu critico curavit D. Eberhard Nestle, novis curis elaboravit D. Erwin Nestle. Editio duodevicesima. Stuttgart: Priviligierte Wurttembergische Bibelanstalt, 1948.

A CHART OF THE PARAGRAPHS IN GALATIANS

According to the American Standard Version (English) and Eberhard Nestle's Text of the Greek New Testament

NO.	REF.	CONTENT	NO.	REF.	CONTENT
	American Standard Version			Nestle's Greek Testament	
1	1:1-5	Salutation	1	1:1-5	Salutation
2	1:6-10	Statement of Occasion	2	1:6-9	Statement of Occasion
3	1:11-17	Paul's First Contacts with the Gospel	3	1:10-2:21	Biographical Statements Concerning Paul
4	1:18-24	Paul's First Travels			
5	2:1-10	Paul's Visit to the Apostles			
6	2:11-21	Interview with Cephas at Antioch			
7	3:1-14	Justification by Faith not by Law	4	3:1-4:7	Contrast of Status Under Grace with Status Under Law
8	3:15-22	Purpose of the Law			
9	3.23-29	The Position of Sonship			
10	4:1-7	The Meaning of Sonship			
11	4:8-11	Contrast with Past	5	4:8-11	Former State as Heathen
12	4:12-20	Personal Appeal	6	4:12-20	Personal Appeal
13	4:21-31	Allegory of Hagar	7	4:21-31	Allegory of Hagar
14	5:1	Transition	8	5:1	Transition
15	5:2-12	Danger of Circumcision	9	5:2-12	Danger of Circumcision
16	5:13-15	Freedom in Love	10	5:13-6:10	Practical Exhortations
17	5:16-24	Moral Fruit of Life in the Spirit			
18	5:25-26	Exhortation to Walk in the Spirit			
19	6:1-5	Practical Life in the Spirit			
20	6:6-10	Sowing and Reaping			
21	6:11-16	Final Personal Appeal	11	6:11-16	Final Appeal
22	6:17	Statement of Personal Feeling	12	6:17	Personal Expression
23	6:18	Final Farewell	13	6:18	Final Farewell

Although the text could well be studied by paragraphs, since each contains a unit of thought, the epistle as a whole cannot be understood unless their organization be made clear. A sequence of paragraphs no more makes a treatise than a collection of lumber, nails, and plaster makes a house. The relationship of the component parts must be established to indicate the outline of thought.

A study of the paragraphs will readily show that Galatians is divisible into five main blocks of text. First is the section comprising the opening salutation and statement of the occasion of the epistle, paragraphs no. 1 and no. 2 (1:1-9). Second is the section which deals with Paul's personal career, paragraphs no. 3 to no. 6 (1:10 to 2:21). This division follows the Greek rather than the English system. The tenth verse of the first chapter and verses 18 to 21 of the second chapter may be parenthetic and transitional; nevertheless they belong in the second block of text.

The third block of text begins with paragraph no. 7, and continues through paragraph no. 10, or possibly through paragraph no. 13. Galatians 3:1, which opens with a challenge to thought, continues with one line of argument through 4:7 anyway, which leaves the reader with a positive conclusion: "So that thou art no longer a bondservant, but a son; and if a son, then an heir through God" (4:7). The text that follows from 4:8-31 inclusive might be classed as a separate block, since it contains largely personal appeal rather than theological argument. On the other hand, all of Galatians is impassioned and personal, so that the criterion of shifting from argument to exhortation does not apply more closely here than it does conversely between 3:6 and 3:7, where there is no paragraph division. Perhaps the most satisfactory solution would be to call 3:1 to 4:31 a block of theological argument, interspersed with exhortation. The symmetry of 4:7, 4:11, 4:20, and 4:31 is apparent when one compares the ends of these successive paragraphs. The first and fourth speak of a settled standing which the believer has attained by right, the privilege which is legally his. The second and third express Paul's fears lest the state of the Galatians should not be the same as their standing. The obvious intent of the third block of text is to present the theological groundwork for the liberty which is the rightful possession of believers.

The fourth block of text begins with paragraph no. 14, which is the transitional verse at 5:1, and continues through paragraph no. 20, ending with 6:10. Two related themes appear in this section: the inward work of the Holy Spirit in the life that has been emancipated from legalism, and the practical ethical effects to be expected in such a life. The urge toward perfection is recognized, and a positive answer is given to the questions raised in 3:1-5.

The three last paragraphs, no. 21 to no. 23 in the English version and no. 11 to no. 13 in the Greek text, form a conclusion which unites personal feeling and the summary of the teaching of the book.

The fourth reading of the book should crystallize the teaching of the various paragraphs into an integrated outline. In Galatians such an outline may be created by organizing the content in topical fashion, using the foregoing blocks as the main divisions. The tenor of the outline will be argumentative rather than descriptive, since the character of the book is essentially polemic.

GALATIANS: The Charter of Christian Liberty[5]

5. For other outlines of Galatians, see B. W. Bacon, *Commentary on the Epistle of Paul to the Galatians* (New York; The Macmillan Company, 1909), pp. 41-43; and Ernest D. Burton, *A Critical and Exegetical Commentary on the Epistle to the Galatians* (New York: Charles Scribner's Sons, 1920) pp. lxxii-lxxiv.

QUESTIONS ABOUT THE BOOK

The Critical Method

CHAPTER II

QUESTIONS ABOUT THE BOOK

The Critical Method

Definition of Method

SOME WORDS in the scholastic vocabulary of Christian thinkers have suffered the fate of the unfortunate man who went down from Jerusalem to Jericho. He fell among thieves, who beat and plundered him, leaving him half dead by the roadside; so that all travellers looked at him askance, and passed by as hurriedly as possible. Such a word is "critical," for it has been associated for so long a time with the methods of study adopted by a hostile rationalism that it has fallen into disrepute in evangelical circles. It is, nevertheless, a good and useful term, and the method which it describes is quite legitimate when it is employed with the proper motives. The critical study of Galatians does not necessarily mean that the text is to be dissected for the purpose of exposing errors in it, but rather that it is being examined in order that the student may ascertain what lies behind it and what evidence it supplies for its own reliability.

Critical study deals with two main fields: historical, or higher criticism, and textual, or lower criticism. The terms "higher" and "lower" do not refer to any particular superiority or inferiority resident in those fields themselves, but rather to the spheres of origin. Lower criticism deals with the transmission of the text of the document under consideration. It seeks to determine whether the text which the original author wrote has been transmitted exactly as he committed it to manuscript, or whether it has suffered changes in copying which have altered or perverted its meaning. Obviously, if the Bible is the

39

Word of God, it is reliable only insofar as its original text has been accurately preserved in the manuscripts and translations now in existence.

Higher criticism concerns itself with the persons, forces, and conditions which led to the production of the text. Its function can best be described by an illustration. Suppose that during the process of cleaning an attic a letter were discovered, purporting to be written by Abraham Lincoln, in which President Lincoln had said that he had just received a radio message from England concerning diplomatic relations with the United States. The letter would be pronounced a forgery immediately, because Lincoln could never have written any such thing, since radio transmission was unknown in the mid-nineteenth century. Similarly, if an ancient document contains a reference which implies a condition or a trend of thought which is known definitely not to have existed in the day when the document was presumably written, it is regarded with suspicion as a possible forgery.

On the other hand, results of critical study need not be negative. Imagine that the aforementioned letter did not contain any glaring anachronism such as the one given above, but that it revealed some previously unknown diplomatic connection between Lincoln and the court of St. James. A careful critical scrutiny might open a whole new realm of historical knowledge which would change completely the current view of the history of Lincoln's period. Thus criticism can strengthen as well as destroy values when it is properly employed. Judgment concerning what may or may not have been written in a certain period should not be limited by ignorance of that period.

The dangers of the critical method, however, should always be kept in mind. When it is employed solely for its own sake in order to invent some new hypothesis of partition, or for the purpose of discrediting a document which contains truth unpalatable to the critic, it is a liability rather than an asset. The critical method of comparing evidence and of deducing conclusions from it is assuredly legitimate. On the other hand, the subjective assumption of what is probable and of what is not probable has entered too much into past study of the Bible. If one presupposes that "miracles do not happen," then historical criticism based on that assumption will reject the truthfulness of much of the New Testament narrative. If objective data are to be cast aside in favor of subjective judgment in the field of textual criticism, as is now being advocated in some circles,[1] then there will no longer be any possibility of finality in the testimony of the manuscripts, to say nothing of any finality in determining what their message is. It may be that hard and fast rules are not always applicable to critical problems; but a fine line should be preserved between private judgment founded on full knowledge and private opinion that is shaped by personal taste and experience. Spiritual truths can only be spiritually discerned; and the attempt to account for them on a purely rationalistic basis is unscholarly as well as futile.

One should always remember that the Biblical documents with which the scholars deal are in themselves firsthand sources of information. The type of criticism which regards them with suspicion just because they are religious, and which commences investigation by looking for faults and discrepancies, is unscientific because it is prejudiced. These documents were not written by falsifiers who put their sentiments on paper for the pure pleasure of fooling a gullible public. On the contrary, they were written by men who had sacrificed comforts, wealth, and reputation, and who had risked life itself for the sake of the gospel which they had espoused. Even apart from the question of inspiration, the writers of the Bible should be cred-

---

1. E. C. Colwell, "Biblical Criticism: Lower and Higher," in *Journal of Biblical Literature* LXVII (1948), p. 5: "In this complexity, the student is guided not by rules, but by knowledge and judgment. He is guided by his knowledge of scribes and manuscripts, of Christian history and institutions and theology, and of the books whose textual form he is striving to perfect. *He is guided by his own judgment, a quality through which the application of reason to knowledge becomes an art.*" (Italics ours)

ited with at least as much sincerity and accuracy as the other writers of antiquity whose claims to truth have not been so drastically analyzed. No scholar, of course, can claim faithfully complete lack of prejudice. Every human being has certain presuppositions of thinking and moves in certain circles of society which affect his mental processes consciously or unconsciously. Absolute impartiality is foreign to human nature. Although this presentation of the critical study of Galatians is avowedly from the evangelical side, it attempts to avoid extravagant claims and unfair misrepresentation of the positions of others.

For the purpose of this chapter, textual criticism will not be treated as a separate topic, though there may be reference to variant readings in the text of Galatians as occasion may require. The approach will be confined to the aspect of historical criticism as it deals with the authorship, unity, destination, occasion, date, and place of writing. The treatment will be relatively brief, since some of the topics will be treated more extensively under other methods of study. In any event, the aim of this work is to be introductory rather than exhaustive in the exposition of Galatians, in order to familiarize the student with methods rather than to furnish an encyclopaedic statement of detail.

The Authorship of Galatians

The first step in a critical appraisal of a book of the Bible is the establishment of authorship. Whom does the book claim for an author? The writing will be worth as much as the author is worth, for only insofar as he is recognized as appointed and inspired of God will his writings carry revelational authority. It may be that, in the last analysis, the books should be regarded as self-authenticating, since in many instances little is known concerning the author beyond what the books themselves have to say. Generally, however, the identification of the author helps to locate the writing in the stream of truth which God has poured out through His chosen servants. If the authorship of a book is uncertain, its authority may be challengeable. The establishment of authority depends upon two kinds of evidence: external and internal. External evidence is derived from sources outside of the document under consideration. Internal evidence is dependent upon the content of the document itself. Both are useful; but in the inductive study of the Biblical text internal evidence is more easily available, and therefore will be stressed here.

Although internal evidence of authorship is scant in some books of the Bible, there is no shortage of it in Galatians. The name of Paul occurs in the salutation (1:1), coupled with his title of apostle. The word *apostle,* meaning "one sent," or "delegate," was the term by which he defined his authority. To him, apostleship was determined by two factors: his personal vision of Christ, and the results of his ministry in soul-winning (I Cor. 9:1, 2). He recognized the fact that *apostle* had become an official term which could be applied to the leaders of the church (I Cor. 9:1), but he did not trade on his rights as an official. He regarded his authority as the privilege rather than as the basis of his service. Since he had served the Galatian people by bringing to them the message of the gospel, he used his apostolic office to demand a respectful hearing for what he still had to say to them.

The name of Paul is not an arbitrary insertion in the first paragraph of Galatians, for it occurs again in the body of this letter (5:2). The personal tone, maintained throughout all of the chapters, indicates that the epistle is the product of one whose individuality and intimate experience are inseparable from the text. Practically all of chapters one and two are autobiographical; the expostulations of chapter three (3:1-6,15) are in the first person singular; the appeals of chapter four refer directly to the relations between the recipients and the author (4:11, 12-20); the intensity of Paul's witness appears in chapter five (5 :2,3) ; and the conclusion in chapter six ends with an allusion to the author's sufferings for Christ (6:17). Galatians is not an essay that might have been written by anybody and ascribed to Paul. It is so warm and intimate that it cannot be separated from the man himself.

Such external evidence as can be found confirms the case for the Pauline authorship. Brief allusions in the writings of the successors of the apostles indicate that it was circulated and used at the beginning of the second century. Polycarp in particular shows some acquaintance with the phraseology of Galatians, though he does not mention it by name. [2] Definite quotations from the epistle are to be found in the writings of Irenaeus of the late second century, who quoted it directly as Pauline, [3] and also in the works of Clement of Alexandria and of Origen, who lived in the half-century following Irenaeus. [4]

Even among the so-called heretics of the second century, such as Marcion, Galatians was recognized as Pauline, and the Muratorian Canon (c. A.D. 180) and Eusebius' list (c. A.D. 325) contain it. It was certainly accepted as genuine in the early church.

---

2. Cf. Polycarp,
To the Philippians 3:2, 3 and Gal. 4:26: "the mother of us all."
To the Philippians 5:1 and Gal. 6:7: "God is not mocked."
To the Philippians 12:2 and Gal. 1:1: "Who shall believe in our Lord Jesus Christ and in his Father who raised him from the dead."
3. Cf. Irenaeus, *Against Heresies,* III :6, 5 — "And the Apostle Paul also, saying, 'For though ye have served them which are no gods, ye now know God, or rather, are known of God . . .'" and Gal. 4:8, 9.
Op. cit. III :7, 2 — "An example occurs in the [Epistle] to the Galatians, where he expresses himself as follows: 'Wherefore then the law of works? It was added, until the seed should come to whom the promise was made; [and it was] ordained by angels in the hand of a Mediator.'" Cf. Gal. 3:19.
4. Clement of Alexandria, *Stromata* III :15 — "Wherefore Paul also, writing to the Galatians, says: 'My little children, with whom I travail in birth again until Christ be formed in you.'" (translated from the Latin text). Cf. Gal. 4:19.
Origen, *Against Celsus,* V :64: "The world is crucified unto me and I unto the world." Cf. Gal. 6:14.
The translated text appears in A. Roberts & J. Donaldson, *op. cit.,* as follows: Polycarp, I, 33, 34, 35; Irenaeus, I, 420; Clement of Alexandria. II, 400; Origen, IV, 571.

Galatians, therefore, with few exceptions, is accepted as Pauline by the conservative and radical critics alike. The Tubingen school, headed by F. C. Baur in the early nineteenth century, were the first to challenge seriously the authorship of any of the Pauline epistles; but they accepted without reservation the genuineness of Galatians. A few writers of the late nineteenth century [5] contended that none of the Pauline epistles were actually written by Paul, and they ascribed them to a Pauline editor or to a late school of Pauline writers. These views have not been taken seriously by the majority of scholars. Burton says that "they belong to the history of opinion rather than to living issues." [6]

The establishment of the Pauline authority of Galatians affords solid ground to the scholar who is seeking to reconstruct an accurate picture of the problems and teachings of the early church, and it gives assurance to the Bible teacher who wants to present the genius of the gospel as it was proclaimed by the preachers of the first century.

The Unity of Galatians

The unity of the epistle is above question. There is no indication whatever that it has ever suffered editorial rearrangement. Its vehemence sometimes transcends the bounds of smooth rhetoric, but from first to last it reflects one author, one occasion, and one purpose. Paul asserted emphatically that he wrote it with his own hand (6:11), as if he would impress his readers with his earnestness and with his emphasis upon the truth which the epistle contained.

------

5. A. D. Loman, *Quaestiones Paulinae* in *Theologisch Tijdschrift,* 1882. A. Pierson and S. A. Naber, *Verisimilia: Laceram conditionem Novi Testamenti exemplia illustrarunt et ab origine repetierunt.*
   R. Steck, *Der Galaterbrief nach seiner Echtheit untersucht.* Berlin, 1888.
   Van Manen, "Paul," in *Encyclopaedia Biblica,* III, col. 3603 ff., esp. cols. 3627 and 3631.

6. Burton, *op. cit.,* pp. lxx, lxxi.

The Destination of Galatians

Who were "the churches of Galatia"?

Historically, the name of Galatia was derived from the Gauls, who invaded central Asia Minor in the third century before Christ, and who established an independent kingdom centered about the cities of Pessinus, Ancyra (the modern Angora), and Tavium. In 64 B.C. after the Roman conquest of the Near East, Pompey divided the territory of Galatia under three chiefs; Amyntas was appointed king of Pisidia and Phrygia; and Polemon was made king of Lycaonia and Isauria. Twenty-eight years later, under the administration of Mark Antony, in 36 B.C., Amyntas was given Galatia and Lycaonia, and at the death of Antony he took over Pamphylia, Cilicia, and Derbe. The territory of the kingdom was thus increased considerably.

In 25 B.C. Amyntas was killed, and the Romans made a new province of Pamphylia. Part of Lycaonia, including Derbe, was given to Archelaus of Cappadocia. In A.D. 41, the boundary of Galatia was Derbe, which was restored to it. Lystra and Antioch were made *coloniae*. The entire province, including both the original territory of the Gauls and the sections that had been added to it were called Galatia. Such was its extent from the days when Barnabas and Paul began evangelizing Asia Minor until Nero in A.D. 63 added the country called Pontus Polemoniacus to the province. This territory included (1) the coast on each side of Amisos in the province Bithynia Pontus; (2) the kingdom of Polemon II; (3) the Galatic territory of Pontus, called Pontus Galaticus.[7] The history of Galatia after the time of Nero does not affect the narrative of the New Testament.

---

7. Sir William Ramsay, *A Historical Commentary on St. Paul's Epistle to the Galatians* (New York: G. P. Putnam's Sons. 1900), p. 123.
   Cf. also *The Cambridge Ancient History*, Vol. X. *The Augustan Empire.* 44 B. C.-A. D. 70. Edited by S. A. Cook, F. E. Aldrich, M. P. Charlesworth. (New York: The Macmillan Company, 1934.) pp. 54, 261, 774.

The name Galatia, then, was applied not only to the original territory possessed by the Gauls located in the north central part of Asia Minor, but was applied also to the entire Roman province which, in Paul's day, comprised a much larger territory extending southward to the borders of Lycia, Pamphylia, and the kingdom of Antiochus. The attempt to define which of these meanings should be given to the name in the New Testament has given rise to the two hypotheses known as the North Galatian and South Galatian theories.

The question concerning the destination of this epistle is whether Paul were using the national name, applicable only to the northern territory, or whether he were using the general provincial name which could mean the southern portion as well.

A study of the New Testament usage shows that the words "Galatia" and "Galatians" occur in seven passages. In Galatians 1:2 the territory is mentioned in the salutation of the epistle, and in 3:1 the people of the churches are addressed directly. Neither of these occurrences is definitive, since it might apply to either theory.

In I Corinthians 16·1 Paul spoke of "the churches of Galatia." He was engaged in raising funds for the poor in Jerusalem, and on a recent visit to Galatia he had requested the churches there to make a contribution. In the same context he referred to Macedonia (16:5), to Achaia (16:15), and to Asia (16:19). Since Achaia, Macedonia, and Asia are the names of Roman provinces, it seems likely that Galatia is also to be taken in this context as a province.

In II Timothy 4:10 Paul makes one allusion to Galatia. The reference is obviously to the province.

The two other passages which contain references to Galatia are found in Acts. The former of the two, Acts 16:6, says: "And they went through the region of Phrygia and Galatia . . ." [8] The expression is peculiar, and could better be translated, "the Phrygian and Galatic region," or "the Phrygio-Galatic country." The interpretation is somewhat complicated by a variant reading[9] which substitutes for the finite verb, "They went through," a participle which would convey a temporal idea: "after they had traversed," or "after they had gone through . . ." Since they were on their way westward, the territory must have been adjacent to Asia and Mysia, which they sought to enter and could not. The second phrase occurs in Acts 18:23: "the region of Galatia and Phrygia in order." [10] Here the Galatian region and Phrygia are treated as two separate regions, traversed in order of mention. In Acts 19:1 Luke said that Paul "having passed through the upper country came to Ephesus." Perhaps he meant by the "Phrygio-Galatic region" the mountainous terrain over which the high roads passed from the central and southern plateau of Asia Minor down to the river valleys of its western slopes.

The Lukan use of these terms thus may or may not coincide with Paul's usage. Paul apparently referred to the province of Galatia as it was in his day, but to which part? Luke used only the adjective, Galatic or Galatian, which may be either ethnic or provincial in its meaning.

A careful consideration of the journeys of Paul shows that in Acts 16:6 a new missionary venture was begun. Paul had completed the revisitation of the churches of Derbe, Lystra, Iconium, and Pisidian Antioch which had been founded on his first journey (Acts 13, 14) and he was looking for new fields of evangelization. He had been "forbidden of the Holy Spirit to speak the word in Asia," and so took the road which passed

8. Greek: *Dielthon de ten Phrygian kai Galatiken choran.*
9. Greek: *Dielthontes.* This reading does not have strong manuscript support. For a full discussion of this point, see K. Lake, *The Earlier Epistles of St. Paul* (London: Rivingtons, 1911), pp. 253-316. He suggests that if *dielthon* is the correct reading, the dependent participle *koluthentes,* "having been forbidden," may be retrospective, in which case they went to Asia first, and went to Galatia as a second choice.
10. Greek: *ten Galatiken choran kai Phrygian.*

through the Phrygio-Galatic territory on his way to Bithynia. If the second reading of 16:6, as given above, should be adopted as correct,[11] then the clause might be taken as equating the Phrygio-Galatic region with the churches of Southern Galatia which he had just visited. In neither case does the language imply necessarily that he made a long journey to the north east into ethnic Galatia.

The language of Acts 18:23 seems to confirm this conclusion. In summarizing the journey from Antioch to Ephesus, Luke said that Paul "established the disciples." It is possible that he was alluding to the disciples who were converts of the second journey in the territory mentioned in 16:6; but it is more likely that he meant the churches of South Galatia which were the first Gentile churches outside of Antioch and which constituted the chief problem in the relation of Jewish and Gentile Christians in the early apostolic age.[12] They needed the "establishment" that Paul could give them.

The identification of the Galatian churches with those founded by Paul on his first journey, and subsequently revisited on the second and third journeys is the substance of the "South Galatian" theory. Paul's use of the term Galatia as provincial could certainly mean that the churches of the epistle are those of the southern cities; and Luke's phraseology does not contradict this conclusion. If Luke's use of the term "Galatic" refers to a particular section of Galatia, it could be possible that Paul visited the northern section on his second and third journeys; but if so, Luke attached little importance to it.

Lightfoot, in his notable commentary on Galatians, contends that "the churches of Galatia" belong to Galatia proper.[13] "There are many reasons," he says, "which make it probable

---

11. The reading *dielthontes* may safely be rejected.
12. Henry C. Thiessen, *Introduction to the New Testament* (Fourth Edition; Grand Rapids, Mich.; Wm. B. Eerdmans Pub. Co., 1948), p. 215. Thiessen notes that Luke did not say "churches."
13. J. B. Lightfoot, *St. Paul's Epistle to the Galatians* (Tenth Edition; London: Macmillan & Co., 1890), pp. 18-35.

that the Galatia of St. Paul and St. Luke is not the Roman province of that name, but the land of the Gauls." He points out that Luke's use of Mysia, Pisidia, and Phrygia is ethnic or geographical, without regard for political divisions; therefore Galatia should be used in similar fashion. Since Luke called Lystra and Derbe cities of Lycaonia, and since he spoke of Antioch as Pisidian, Lightfoot feels that they cannot be considered as Galatian towns. He suggested that perhaps Luke's comparative silence concerning the Galatian churches was caused by their early defection, and that the subject was either too painful to discuss, or else that they were relatively unimportant in the development of Gentile Christianity in the first century.

Luke, however, did not always avoid painful subjects, as the episode of the parting between Barnabas and Paul shows (Acts 15:36-40); and it is hard to understand why he would have omitted any reference to the Galatian controversy when he discussed at such length the dispute which took place in Antioch and Jerusalem at the end of the first journey. Furthermore, the references to Barnabas in Galatians seem almost inexplicable unless the churches of Galatia refer to those founded on the first journey, since Barnabas did not travel with Paul through the "region of Phrygia and Galatia" (Acts 16:6).

The only other mention of Galatians in the New Testament is in I Peter 1:1, where the term is used in a purely political sense. It occurs in conjunction with several other names of political or geographical origin, all of which are provincial rather than ethnic in character.

In interpreting the Scripture by these two rival theories, one should remember that their value is solely critical and historical. Neither theory affects the doctrinal truth of Galatians, and each has something to be said in its favor, for the evidence is not all on one side.

The North Galatian theory is the older of the two. It assumes that Paul's visit to Galatia began on the second journey
when he left the southern territory of Derbe, Lystra, and Iconium, and traveled through "the region of Phrygia and Galatia"
mentioned in Acts 16:6. The defenders of this view hold that
he traversed the territory of old Galatia, Pessinus, possibly
Ancyra and Tavium, and then finally reached Troas after a
long journey. A return trip on the third journey is predicated
by the language of Acts 18:23, which says that he "went
through the region of Galatia, and Phrygia, in order, establishing all the disciples." This was generally the view of such
commentators as Davidson,[14] Godet,[15] Lightfoot,[16] Moffatt,[17]
and is still held by some writers of the present day.

The South Galatian theory holds that all references to Galatia in the Pauline epistles concern the province as a whole,
and that the Galatian churches are those of the cities which
Acts expressly names in Paul's travels, Derbe, Lystra, Iconium, and Pisidian Antioch. The chief advocate of the theory
was Sir William Ramsay, whose archaeological researches in
Asia Minor made him an authority on the subject. Most modern commentators, such as Bacon,[18] Burton,[19] Duncan,[20] Emmet,[21] and others, agree that this epistle is addressed to the
churches of South Galatia. The strength of this hypothesis
depends on several considerations:

14. Samuel Davidson, *An Introduction to the Study of the New Testament,* (Second Edition Revised and Improved; London: Longmans, Green
& Co., 1882), I, 70, 72.
15. F. Godet, *Introduction to the New Testament,* I, *The Epistles of
St. Paul,* (Translated from the French by William Affleck; Edinburgh:
T. & T. Clark, 1894) pp. 182-188.
16. J. B. Lightfoot, *op. cit.,* pp. 18-22.
17. James Moffatt, *An Introduction to the Literature of the New Testament* (New York: Charles Scribner's Sons, 1911), pp. 90-101.
18. Benjamin W. Bacon, *op. cit.,* pp. 17-24.
19. Ernest D. Burton, *op. cit.,* pp. xxix-xliv
20. George S. Duncan, *The Epistle of Paul to the Galatians,* (New York:
Harper & Bros., Publishers, n.d.) pp. xviii-xxi.
21. Cyril W. Emmet, *St. Paul's Epistle to the Galatians,* (New York·
Funk & Wagnalls, 1916), pp. ix-xiv.

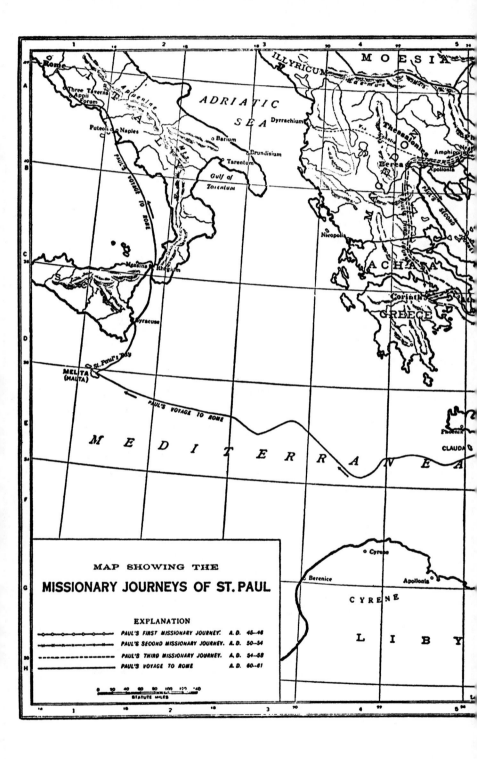

MAP SHOWING THE

MISSIONARY JOURNEYS OF ST. PAUL

EXPLANATION

—o—o—o—o—	PAUL'S FIRST MISSIONARY JOURNEY.	A.D. 45--46
—x—x—x—x—	PAUL'S SECOND MISSIONARY JOURNEY.	A.D. 50--54
------------	PAUL'S THIRD MISSIONARY JOURNEY.	A.D. 54--58
————————	PAUL'S VOYAGE TO ROME	A.D. 60--61

STATUTE MILES

1. The cities mentioned above which Paul visited on his first journey were all within the province of Galatia at the time when the recorded evangelization took place.

2. There is no record of any extended preaching or of any organization of churches in the North Galatian territory. If Luke's allusions to "Phrygia and Galatia" in Acts 16:6 and 18:23 refer to North Galatia, Paul's visit was casual, and the "establishing of all the disciples" seemingly implies that he dealt with individuals rather than with organized groups.

3. The main roads from Cilicia to the Aegean coast did not pass through North Galatia. The logical route for Paul to follow on his second journey would take him from Tarsus north through the Cilician Gates, then westward through Derbe and Lystra, then northward to Iconium, and thence westward to Pisidian Antioch. The "region of Phrygia and Galatia" lay to the north and west of Antioch. Evidently Paul did turn northward at this point, but the account given in Acts 16:6-8 indicates that he did not turn eastward into the cities of North Galatia, but westward toward Mysia until he reached Troas. If the phrase in 16:6 is to be translated "the Phrygio-Galatic region" as Emmet [22] and others suggest, it probably refers to the Phrygian territory included in the province of Galatia, or else to the territory bordering both Phrygia and Galatia which lay immediately to the west of the province.

4. The presence of Judaizing agitators in the northern cities is less probable than their presence in the southern cities. The latter lay on the direct routes of travel between Palestine and the Aegean ports, and a Jewish population is specifically mentioned in Pisidian Antioch and in Iconium (Acts 13:14, 14:1). The other two cities were accessible to the Jews, since the latter came down to Lystra from Iconium in order to incite the

---

22. *Ibid.* See pp. xii, xiii. On this point Emmet says "The fact that the definite article is not repeated suggests that the phrase means 'the Phrygian and Galatic district,' *Phrygian* being an adjective. It then refers to the district which is both Phrygia and Galatia, i.e the part of Phrygia which belonged to the province of Galatia."

multitude against Paul (14:19). Since some of the converts of this region were Jews and Gentile proselytes, it is only natural to suppose that they would be susceptible to Jewish influence after their conversion. The Jewish influence on the churches of Galatia can be accounted for more easily by assuming that they are identical with these South Galatian churches.

A fair compromise between the two views is advocated by Thiessen, who, in his *Introduction to the New Testament* suggests that the Galatian epistle was directed to the churches of South Galatia, since Paul uniformly employs the term Galatia as a provincial designation; but that the Lukan narrative in Acts refers to visits to northwest Galatia in which the writer did not participate and of which there was little to be reported.[23]

The Occasion for Writing Galatians

The occasion of the epistle is plainly stated in the introduction (1:1-10). Paul had preached to the Galatians, and a number had been converted. The message which he preached was no different from his message in any other place; for he had proclaimed "Jesus Christ . . . crucified" (3:1) and "raised from the dead" (1:1). This message constituted his essential gospel, as he himself stated in I Corinthians 1:23 and 15:1-11. The Galatians had accepted his preaching, and had adhered to it up to the time that he left them.

Subsequent to his departure, however, they lapsed from their new found faith. They accepted a "different" gospel which was not "another" of the same kind.[24] It had been preached by certain persons who were "troubling" or upsetting them, and who were desirous of "perverting" the gospel of Je-

---

23. H. C. Thiessen, *op. cit.*, pp. 214-216.
24. Gal. 1:6, 7. Two different words are used here: *heteros* in vs. 6 means "another" in the sense of one that is different in quality; *allos* in vs. 7 means "another" in the sense of difference in numerical identity. For a discussion of the two terms, see R. C. Trench, *Synonyms of the New Testament*, (Tenth Edition, Corrected and Improved; Grand Rapids, Mich.: Wm. B. Eerdmans Publishing Co., 1948), pp. 358-361.

sus Christ. The idea in the word "perverting" is stronger than distortion; it means reversal.[25] Paul's anger was aroused, not because he was jealous of rivals, but because the leaders of the dissenting party in Galatia were palming off a substitute for the gospel of Christ as the genuine article. His intolerance was not the symptom of bigotry, for he included himself in the imprecation, "Though we, or an angel from heaven, should preach unto you any gospel other than that which we preached unto you, let him be anathema" (1:8). The defection, then, was not merely a difference in theological opinion, but was fundamental to the whole concept of the gospel.

Whether these heterodox leaders were invaders from the outside, or whether they arose from among the Galatians themselves is not clearly stated here. The implied analogy between them and the "certain that came from James" (Gal. 2:12) may suggest that they belonged to a Jewish group who made a business of following Paul and of proselytizing his churches to a legalistic faith. The glamour of their reasoning had "bewitched" (3:1) the Galatians. Evidently those teachers promised perfection through the keeping of the ceremonial law (3:3), which involved the observance of "days, and months, and seasons, and years" (4:10), such as the Galatians had known in their former paganism (4:8). The chief demand on the part of those teachers was circumcision, which, they contended, was symbolic of keeping the law of God (5:2, 3, 6). They had succeeded in persuading the churches of Galatia to accept their demands, with the result that the basic faith of the latter was perverted so that salvation was coming to be regarded as something to be earned rather than as a gift of grace (5:3, 4).

There are present some hints that Paul's personal ministry had been attacked. In 1:10 he said: "For am I now seeking the favor of men, or of God? or am I striving to please men? If I were still pleasing men, I should not be a servant of

---

25. J. B. Lightfoot, *op. cit.*, p. 77. Cf. James 4:9.

Christ." His opponents had insinuated that Paul's readiness
to drop the legal requirements of circumcision and of ceremonial observances was prompted more by a desire to please the
laxity of human nature than by a passion for salvation by faith
in God alone. He was accused of being a preacher of second-
hand truth which he had picked up from the apostles of Jesus,
and had misrepresented because of his ignorance (1:11, 16,
17). They may have said that he had been repudiated by the
Jerusalem church; for Paul went out of his way to state that
the leaders of the church had given to him the right hand of
fellowship and that they had approved of his work (2:9).
Others, inconsistently enough, whispered that he was still
preaching circumcision, perhaps when he was not among the
Gentiles (5:11).

If Galatians were not written until after the second journey, some plausibility was lent to this last accusation of Paul's
opponents by his circumcision of Timothy. Since Timothy was
half Gentile, the Judaizers could point to this instance as
Paul's violation of his own principle. Acts 16:3 states that
Paul did so as a definite concession to the Jews of the region
of Lystra and Iconium. He was not contending that Jewish
believers repudiate circumcision, but only that Gentile believers
should not be compelled to adopt it for themselves.

Paul met the accusations with a spirited denial, supported by
the biographical and theological facts contained in this epistle.
The argument of Galatians, however, is no tempest in a theological teapot nor an unimportant record of a personal quar-
rel. In the dispute within the Galatian churches the entire
question of Christian liberty was at stake. Spontaneous spiritual life versus legalism, salvation by works versus salvation
by grace, ceremonialism versus the activity of a creative faith
were the alternate forces battling for supremacy. Galatians,
as Paul himself indicated, is the presentation of the gospel of
Christ, salvation by faith, and by faith in Him alone.

The Date of Galatians

Another critical problem connected with Galatians is its date. Two general termini between which it was written may be fixed with a high degree of certainty. The *terminus a quo,* the point after which it must have been written, was at least as late as the date of the close of the first missionary journey, since Paul had not visited Galatia at all prior to that time according to the existing records. The actual date of his visit or visits to Galatia depends somewhat upon whether one assumes the North or the South Galatian theory as correct; but in either case it could hardly have been prior to A.D. 47. [26] The *terminus ad quem* would at the latest be Paul's death; but since he seems to have been still free to travel when he wrote,[27] one may conclude that the epistle was written before his detention and imprisonment at Jerusalem (Acts 21:33 ff). Since that imprisonment took place about A.D. 58, it seems most likely that Galatians should be placed somewhere within the decade which elapsed between the dates given above.

Since a thorough analysis of all the factors relative to this question would involve material that rightfully should be treated in other chapters of this work, the problem of the date will be stated concisely rather than exhaustively at this point; and such pertinent evidence as appears in the main body of Galatians will be mentioned later.

Three possible dates have been suggested for the writing of Galatians. The first places its composition at the end of Paul's first missionary journey, just prior to the Council of Jerusa-

---

26. A. D. 47 is the dating of Harnack, which C. H. Turner thinks is too early. See "New Testament Chronology," in J. Hastings, *Dictionary of the Bible* (New York: Charles Scribner's Sons, 1902), I, 424b. David Smith, *The Life and Letters of St. Paul* (New York: George H. Doran, n.d.), p. 649, places the return to Syrian Antioch in midsummer of A. D. 49, but dates the writing of the letter in A. D. 53.
27. Cf. Gal. 5:11, which assumes that he is still preaching. No mention is made of imprisonment. While the argument from silence is not conclusive, it is probable that had Paul been confined, he would have made some allusion to the fact as he did in his later epistles. See Eph. 3:1, 4:1; Phil. 1:7, 12, 13, 17; Col. 4:3; Philemon 1:8-10, 22.

lem which was held about the years, A.D. 48, 49. The arguments for the early date are as follows:

1. The churches to which this epistle was addressed were acquainted with Barnabas, and, by reputation at least, with Peter (2:1, 9, 13; 2:9, 11). This would probably have been true only of the churches of South Galatia, since Barnabas did not go with Paul on the second and third journeys

2. If the churches of South Galatia only are concerned, and if the schism within these churches occurred later than the Jerusalem Council in A. D. 48, why did not Paul settle the question easily by quoting the decrees of the Council, as Acts 16:4 states that he actually did on his second visit?

3. Why should the episode with Cephas in Antioch have occurred after the Council? On the assumption of the identity of Peter and Cephas, it seems incredible that he should have been so fearful of criticism from the Judaistic party as 2:12 intimates. Furthermore, "even Barnabas was carried away with their dissimulation" (2:13), and since Barnabas and Paul separated after the Council, the whole course of events narrated in Galatians 1:11 to 2:13 must have taken place prior to or synchronously with the Council.

4. The language of 1:6 indicates surprise on Paul's part that the defection had come as quickly as it had. The text does not say whether Paul had observed the defection while present in Galatia and had written the letter after leaving, or whether he wrote because of news that had been brought to him. The latter seems to be the case; for in 3:1 he says. "Who did bewitch you?" as though he were unacquainted personally with those responsible for the schism. If Paul means "so quickly" (1:6) that the Galatians' lapse came shortly after their initial conversion, then it may well be that upon returning to Antioch he learned of the sad state of affairs, and wrote this letter to check the drift toward legalism.

5. An early dating[28] places this controversy at the time when the whole issue of the relation of the Gentile believer to the requirements of the Mosaic law was being discussed in the mother churches of Antioch and Jerusalem. By the end of the second journey the issue was quite well settled as far as Gentile relations were concerned. It is true that James raised a question with Paul concerning the attitude of Jewish believers toward him as late as A.D. 56 or 58; but the question was not then one of Paul's principles, to which James was evidently reconciled, but to Paul's practice as misunderstood by the Jewish believers of the Diaspora.

If, then, Galatians be dated in A.D. 47 or 48, certain results follow:

1. The total silence of Paul concerning the decrees of the Council of Jerusalem can be readily explained.

2. The vividness of the narrative in chapters 1 and 2 is understandable because of the comparative recency of the events described.

3. Galatians becomes the earliest of Paul's extant written epistles, and serves as a polemic exposition of the principle which he enunciated in his preaching as recorded in Acts 13: 38, 39:

> *Be it known unto you therefore, brethren, that through this man is proclaimed unto you remission of sins: and by him everyone that believeth is justified from all things, from which ye could not be justified by the law of Moses.*

There are, however, certain objections to a date as early as A.D. 48.

1. In Galatians 4:13, Paul said: "Ye know that because of an infirmity of the flesh I preached the gospel unto you the first

---

28. The very early date for Galatians is advocated by several modern scholars. D. B. Knox has made a good case for it in "The Date of the Epistle to the Galatians," *Evangelical Quarterly,* XII (1941), 262-268.

time." The word "first" [29] is strictly "former," and implies
the former of two occasions. It is used four times in the
Pauline writings and three times in the book of Hebrews. In
all of the instances other than here, it may have the denotation
of "previously," "formerly." If it is interpreted directly in
4:13, it means the former of two visits, which would imply
that Galatians was written after the second journey.

2. A stronger objection is the chronology given in Galatians
1 and 2. If the figures for time are successive, even allowing for counting fractional years as full years, the book cannot have been written less than fifteen years after Paul's conversion; and it is more than likely that an appreciably longer
time had elapsed. Unless Galatians were written almost immediately after the argument with Peter at Antioch, there
would scarcely be time before A.D. 48 for the occurrence of
all the events implied in this context. Would the Judaizers
have accomplished their work, and would tidings have come
back to Antioch in so short a time?

3. The chief obstacle to the early date is the nature of the
interview at Jerusalem. With what event in Acts should it
be synchronized? If it is identical with the "famine visit" of
Acts 11:27-30, 12:25, there is not time for the lapse of the
years mentioned above; and if it is to be identified with a private view of the Council of Acts 15, then how could Paul say
that in the interim he was "unknown by face unto the churches
of Judea which were in Christ" (1:22)? The "famine visit,"
under this interpretation, is not mentioned in Galatians.

---

29. Greek: *to proteron,* which occurs in II Cor. 1:15, Gal. 4:13, Eph.
4:22, I Tim. 1:13, and Heb. 4:6, 7:27, 10:32. David Smith, *op. cit.,* 653,
says: "Had Paul been in Galatia when he said *euenggelisamen humin,*
then *to proteron* (Anglicizing ours) would have implied only one previous
visit: 'I preached to you on the former occasion, the last time I was here';
but since he was writing to *Galatia,* it implies two previous visits: 'I
preached to you on the former of the two occasions when I visited you.'
Hence the letter was written before the third visit in autumn 53."

If the visit to Jerusalem recorded in Galatians 2 is identical with the Jerusalem Council of Acts 15, then a median date is preferable. Zahn propounds one between A.D. 52 and 54.[30] Before the close of the year A.D. 52 Paul had settled in Corinth for a stay of eighteen months (Acts 18:11) lasting up to the summer of A.D. 54. Zahn holds that Galatians was written from Corinth during this time, either during the absence of Silas and Timothy in Macedonia, or else after they had returned to Macedonia with the Thessalonian letter. In his opinion the former alternative is preferable.

The late date for Galatians, A.D. 55 to 57, is advocated by a large number of scholars. It obviates all chronological difficulties by allowing more than sufficient time for the occurrence of the events of Galatians 1 and 2 between the conversion of Paul and the writing of the epistle. Again, while the two former dates depend upon the acceptance of the South Galatian theory, the late date is reconcilable with either theory of the destination. Another argument frequently advanced for the late date is the similarity of Galatians to Romans. Because of the literary affiliation, it is supposed that both must have been written in the same period. On the contrary, Moffatt comments that "The similarity of attitude in Galatians and Romans yields no safe inference as to their period of composition." [31]

Probably no final date will ever be accepted by all scholars, since so many doubtful factors are involved in reaching any decision. The book of Galatians represents the essence of the Pauline theology, and its content can be traced back to the earliest period of his preaching. The epistles of Paul are not random collections of ideas produced carelessly on the spur of

30. T. Zahn, *Introduction to the New Testament* (Three volumes; New York: Charles Scribner's Sons, 1909), I, pp. 196, 197. B. W. Bacon in his *Introduction to the New Testament* (New York: The Macmillan Co., 1924), p. 57 concurs with Zahn's judgment. His whole chronology is two years earlier than Zahn's, and so coincides with it relatively.
31. Moffatt, *op. cit.*, p. 105.

the moment, but are the applications of principles well thought out and integral to his spiritual experience. The applications vary widely in content and method, but the principles beneath them remain the same. Galatians and Romans contain the same substance of theology, though the former is written like the rebuttal to a debate and the latter is written as an essay.

The Place of Writing

There is no greater agreement among scholars on the place of writing than there is on the date, and Galatians contains no statement to aid in making a decision. If Galatians were written as late as A.D. 57, it was probably composed during Paul's stay in Ephesus after leaving Galatia (Acts 18:23; 19:1, 10),[32] or in Macedonia,[33] or in Corinth,[34] or at Antioch.[35] An acceptance of the median date would make plausible the theory of Bacon and Zahn [36] that it was written from Corinth. If, however, the early date be accepted, Galatians was probably written from Antioch just prior to the Council of Jerusalem.[37] The allusions to Antioch in the body of the epistle seem quite natural if one assumes that Paul was writing from that place, and the abruptness with which he dropped the historical narrative at the end of chapter 2 can be readily explained if he were writing about an occurrence which had just happened in the place where he was.

32. B. Weiss, *A Manual of Introduction to the New Testament* (Translated from the German by A. J. K. Davidson; New York: Funk and Wagnalls, n.d.), I, p. 241.

33. D. Hayes, *Paul and His Epistles* (New York: Methodist Book Concern, 1915), p. 282.

34. W. J. Conybeare and J. S. Howson, *Life and Epistles of St. Paul* (New Edition; Grand Rapids, Mich., Wm. B. Eerdmans Pub. Co., 1949) p. 833.

35. E. J. Goodspeed, *An Introduction to the New Testament* (Chicago: University of Chicago Press, 1937), p. 26.

36. See footnote 30.

37. C. T. Wood, *The Life, Letters, and Religion of St. Paul* (Edinburgh: T. & T. Clark, 1925), p. 73.

By way of summary it may be said that while the critical inspection of Galatians reveals many contradictory inferences concerning the time and place of its composition, its genuineness, unity, and authenticity remain unimpaired. In spite of technical difficulties, this study favors an early production of the book in Syrian Antioch, though such a conclusion cannot be drawn with absolute finality.

THE MAN BEHIND GALATIANS

THE BIOGRAPHICAL METHOD

CHAPTER III

THE MAN BEHIND GALATIANS

THE BIOGRAPHICAL METHOD

G ALATIANS is an excellent illustration of the principle that Christian truth can never be disassociated completely from the personality who is preaching it. Not only does the book show the unconscious accord between Paul's life and his message, but it depends largely for its argument upon the experiential values which he introduced freely from his own background. He presented his autobiography as a defense against the slanderous charge of his opponents that he was only a time-server who was attempting to curry popular favor by diluting the requirements of God's righteous law to a milk-and-water faith that had no duties attached. Nor was the issue entirely concerned with his personal character; for his authority had been challenged also. The gospel which he preached, said the Judaizers, was his own invention, a purely human production. It did not have the weight of the law which was the word of God spoken at Sinai. Why, they argued, should this upstart Tarsian Jew, who was avowedly disloyal to the law and who was not one of the original twelve apostles, be credited with speaking an authoritative message?

The Biographical Approach

In studying the material available in the biographical section of Galatians, which comprises chapters 1:11 to 2:21, plus scattered references in other sections, two lines of approach may be followed: the biographical narrative, as a condensed account of events in Paul's life, and the biographical argument, which attempts to answer the slanders of his enemies. This method of study should include (1) the collection of all the biographical facts in the text of the document under consideration; (2) the comparison with that document of all available facts from other sources; and (3) the careful analysis and interpretation of these facts as they relate to the main theme of the book as a whole.

The Biographical Narrative: Paul

The chief sources of knowledge of Paul's life are the Lukan account in Acts of his persecuting activities, of his conversion, and of his travels; his own speeches, in which he alluded to his early days; and the epistles themselves in which he made casual references to his circumstances, feelings, and plans. Galatians affords more information concerning his career up to the time of its composition than does any other of his writings. The text, therefore, supplemented by cross references to the other sources, should provide the narrative foundation for the biographical argument.

The first stage in Paul's autobiography was his past life in Judaism (1:13), which was not, like so many of the faiths of the Roman world, a veneer that could be put on at will. Through its legal and ceremonial regulations it involved every moment and every act of waking life. To be a Jew meant not only that a man had a religion peculiar to himself, but also that he lived a life that marked him as different from all other men. Paul was born a Jew, though he lived in a Gentile city. In his epistle to the Philippians he said that he was "circumcised the eighth day, of the stock of Israel, of the tribe of Benjamin, a Hebrew of Hebrews" (Phil. 3:5). Both in Galatians and in Philippians his stress on the circumstances of his birth was occasioned by the accusation that he was not a true Jew. He replied that he bore the marks of circumcision, the permanent outward symbol of submission to the law. He

was not born of proselyte stock, but his ancestors before him
were Jewish, and belonged to "Israel," the term that Paul used
whenever he wished to refer to the spiritually alert core of the
nation (Rom. 2:28, 29; 9:6-9; 11:1), or when he stressed the
spiritual nature of their material heritage. His reference to
Benjamin was doubtless prompted by the natural pride in the
reputation for valor which that tribe possessed. Though it
was one of the smallest of the original twelve tribes (Num.
2:22, 23; I Sam. 9:21), and though it was disowned and almost extirpated by the other tribes in the period of the Judges
following the conquest (Judges 20:12-48), it was restored ultimately to its rightful place in Israel (Judges 21). Saul, the
first king of Israel, for whom Paul was doubtless named, was
a Benjamite (I Sam. 9:1); and the Benjamites gave good account of themselves in the early warfare of the united kingdom (I Chron. 8:40; 12: 2). By referring to such ancestry
Paul reminded his enemies that he came of "fighting blood."

Paul's claim to being a "Hebrew of Hebrews" (Phil.
3:5) refers to the atmosphere and type of his home life. Although he was a native of Tarsus, a Greek city which was a
cosmopolitan seaport and a university center, his family had
not become thoroughly Hellenized. Evidently Paul's father had
retained the use of the Aramaic tongue, so that Paul learned
it in childhood and could speak it fluently; for he addressed
in Aramaic the Jews who had assaulted him at Jerusalem upon his return from his third journey (Acts 21:27, 40). Many
of the Jews of the Dispersion, though they were quite con-
scious of their Jewish descent and although they had retained
many of the ancestral beliefs, had adopted the Greek language
and Gentile manners, much as the Reformed Jew of the present day has adopted national customs in the place of those
retained by Orthodox Jewry. The analogy is not exact, since
Reformed Judaism today is less strict in its observance of
the law than were the Hellenistic Jews of the first century.
Then as now there was a wide variation in the rigidity with

which the law was observed. The chief difference between the Hellenists and the Hebrews seems to have been in language and in customs; for the Hebrews retained the use of Hebrew or Aramaic in their worship and in their household life. The widespread use of the Septuagint in the first century is good proof that Judaism was rapidly becoming Hellenized. Paul, of course, spoke Greek, and was conversant with Gentile thought; but he disavowed the tacit implication that his message was the byproduct of Hellenistic influence. Because of his early training he owed his mental and emotional background to the Pentateuch rather than to the philosophers. He was first and foremost a Jew.

In the interpretation of the law Paul was a Pharisee. The statement in Philippians accords exactly with Galatians 1:14 that "I was exceedingly zealous for the traditions of my fathers." Pharisaism is today a synonym for cant and for hypocritical religious austerity. Any religious system which demands of its followers a strictness that transcends the average moral performance of humanity is likely to have adherents who will pretend to be what they are not, in order to maintain a favorable impression among their compatriots. Unquestionably the Pharisees as a class deserved the strictures which Jesus pronounced against them. Nevertheless, Pharisaism did possess some commendable virtues. In speaking to His disciples, Jesus said: "Except your righteousness shall exceed *the righteousness* of the scribes and Pharisees, ye shall in no wise enter into the kingdom of heaven" (Matt. 5:20). By His statement He admitted that the Pharisees had a standard of righteousness, even though He deemed it insufficient for His own disciples.

The Pharisees were, in fact, the backbone of Judaism, and the progenitors of modern Jewish orthodoxy. They were supernaturalists, believing in spiritual reality and in personal immortality, which the more sophisticated and worldly-minded Sadducees rejected (Acts 23:8). Pharisees were eager students of the law, and were keenly interested in each new teaching that bore any relation to it (John 1:19, 24; 3:1, 2; Matt. 22:34). When Jesus uttered His most drastic condemnation of them, He admitted that they spoke the truth (Matt. 23:1-3); but He challenged them because they failed to match their performance to their knowledge. They were active in their proselyting(Matt. 23:15), meticulous in their attempt to avoid evil (23:16-22), and scrupulous in their tithing (23:23). Paul shared the religious zeal of the Pharisees, and undoubtedly would have merited in common with them both Jesus' praise and His condemnation.

Paul's training was received at Jerusalem in the school of Gamaliel, a rabbi renowned for his learning and for his liberal attitude toward his students (Acts 22:3). His attitude toward the apostles as recorded in Acts 5:34-39 indicates that he was no blind partisan, but that he had a healthy respect for truth and a willingness to investigate a new situation before he passed judgment upon it. He allowed his pupils to read Greek literature, and seemed to have a genuine appreciation for the best in Gentile culture. He was, however, a strict Jew; and the Mishna says that "with the death of Gamaliel the reverence for the law ceased, and purity and abstinence died away." [1]

From this teacher Paul may have imbibed his wide knowledge of the Hebrew Scriptures and traditions, his knowledge of rabbinical methods of interpretation, and his appreciation of Greek poets whom he quoted on at least three occasions.[2] He may not have possessed Gamaliel's breadth of judgment, for youth is often likely to absorb the enthusiasm of its elders without taking their caution. He was a promising pupil, for he asserted, "I advanced in the Jews' religion beyond many of mine own age among my countrymen, being more exceeding-

---

1. *Sota* IX, 15, quoted by G. Milligan in "Gamaliel," HDB II, 106b.
2. Acts 17:28: Aratus *Phaenomena* 5; I Cor. 15:33: Menander *Thais;* Titus 1:12: Epimenides *De Oraculis.*

ly zealous for the traditions of my fathers" (Gal. 1:14). He may well have been regarded as the brightest young scholar of Gamaliel's seminary, and as a possible successor for Gamaliel's position of leadership.

There can be no question of Paul's sincerity in his opposition to Christianity in his early life. He made persecution an official career, for he obtained letters from the chief priests in order that he might arrest the Christians in the cities outside of Jerusalem (Acts 9:2; 22:5; 26:10, 11). He felt that he "ought to do many things contrary to the name of Jesus of Nazareth" (Acts 26:9). He measured his zeal as a Jew by the fact that he had persecuted the church, and added that he had been, "as touching the righteousness which is in the law, found blameless" (Phil. 3:6). His subsequent verdict on this period of his life was that he had acted "ignorantly in unbelief" (I Tim. 1:13); but he never admitted that he had been a hypocrite. On the contrary, when he was brought before the high command in Jerusalem to answer for the disturbance which he had caused in the city, he said, "I have lived before God in all good conscience until this day" (Acts 23:1).

Paul's conversion, which was the pivot of his entire career, received less attention in Galatians than might be expected. No details are given such as are found in the threefold account in Acts (9:1-9, 22:5-11, 26:12-20). The supernatural aspect of it, however, is strongly emphasized. "God," he said, "separated me . . . called me" (Gal. 1:15). The entire change in his life he attributed directly to divine intervention and he explained it as the result of God's predetermination to reveal His Son in him. Paul did not choose arbitrarily a new channel for his activities, nor was his conversion the result of a sudden whim nor even of a belated insight into a truth previously neglected. It was the result of a new spiritual vision which only God could give (1:12). When Paul spoke of the veil which covers the hearts of Israel at the reading of the Old Testament (II Cor. 3:14, 15), he must have had his own experience in mind. In his life God had taken the initiative, and had revealed Himself to Paul much as He had dealt with Moses at the burning bush (Exod. 3:2ff.).

The divine intervention consisted of two stages marked by the verbs "separated" and "called." "Separated" refers to the providence of God in ordering his entire career from his birth. It implies that even before his birth his destiny was marked, and that during all of his life before conversion God had been preparing him for his ministry. Such divine procedure has adequate precedent in the Old Testament; for in choosing Jeremiah God said to him,

> *Before I formed thee in the belly I knew thee, and before thou camest forth out of the womb I sanctified thee; I have appointed thee a prophet unto the nations.*
> (Jer. 1:5)

The term which Paul used to express this separation unto God appears in one other passage in his epistles, where he says that he has been "separated unto the gospel of God" (Rom. 1:1). There the word is of positive import: separated "to" rather than separated "from." It denotes the realization of God's purpose as the use of the same term in Galatians denotes the beginning of the execution of that purpose.

"Called" means a definite summons to action. Prior to Paul's conversion, God had been guiding his steps all unknown to him. At his conversion, God came into the foreground of his life, and took the central place in his consciousness and plans. From that time on, Paul, the strict and bigoted Pharisee, became an apostle to the Gentiles, and the advocate of a gospel of liberty that transcended law.

The explanation of this amazing transformation lies in the fact that the conversion was a revelation of Christ. Galatians stresses the purpose of the experience: "to reveal His Son in me" (Gal. 1:16). The accounts in Acts stress its content. The voice which called to him on the Damascus road said: "Saul, Saul, why persecutest thou me? . . . I am Jesus, whom

thou persecutest" (Acts 9:4, 5). The vision made an instant
link between the facts about the historical Jesus of whom Paul
had heard and the faith in the risen Christ which the early believers had manifested, notably Stephen. The light which
blinded Paul and the voice which he heard were objective realities which he could not deny, and which were corroborated
by competent witnesses (Acts 9:7, 22:9).[3] The consequent
conversation between Paul and Christ produced a change in
his life which was subjectively real, and which he always regarded afterward as the most important event of his whole
career. Several of his other epistles contain some allusion to
this event. "God," he wrote in II Corinthians 4:6, "shined in
our hearts, to give the light of the knowledge of the glory of
God in the face of Jesus Christ."[4]

Subsequent to his conversion, Paul retired from public life,
and "went away into Arabia" (Gal. 1:17). Concerning this
trip the book of Acts says nothing, and the duration of the
visit is uncertain. Galatians affirms that three years elapsed
between Paul's conversion and his return to Jerusalem, within which time the journey to Arabia was included. The account of this period is not fully given by Luke; for Acts tells
only of his ministry in Damascus. The visit to Arabia probably occurred during the interval between his conversion and
the return to Jerusalem, though it was not mentioned. Whether it preceded the preaching in the synagogues, and so took
so little time that Luke could say "straightway" (Acts 9:20),
or whether it took place during the "many days" (9:23) prior

---

3. The apparent discrepancy in the accounts between Acts 9:7, which
says that "the men . . . stood speechless, hearing the voice," and Acts 22:9,
"but they heard not the voice of him that spake to me," may be explained
on the assumption that they heard a sound which they recognized as a
voice but which to them seemed inarticulate. Cf. A. T. Robertson, *A Grammar of the Greek New Testament in the Light of Historical Research*
(Third Edition: New York: George H. Doran Co., 1919), p. 506: "But it is
perfectly proper to appeal to the distinction in the cases in the apparent
contradiction between *akouontes men tes phones* (Acts 9:7) and *ten de
phonen ouk ekousan* (22:9)."

4. See also I Cor. 9:1; 15:7-10; Eph. 3:1-8; Phil. 3:7-9; I Tim. 1:12-16.

to his departure from Damascus is uncertain. Nor is it certain what Paul was doing in Arabia. The usual assumption has been that he went there for the purpose of reorganizing his thought. Prior to his conversion he had been a thoroughgoing Pharisee and legalist. To his way of thinking, Jesus was at best a human being, and at worst an impostor. After his conversion he became a champion of Gentile liberty, and he preached Jesus "that he is the Son of God" (Acts 9:20). If Paul made so sudden a shift from Pharisaic legalism to Christianity, and from despising Jesus as an impostor to worshiping Him as deity, it is obvious that such an astounding mental somersault must have been attended by far-reaching effects. A man as thoughtful as Paul could scarcely have reversed his entire religious position overnight without having considered carefully at least some of the consequences of his decision. According to his own testimony, he was committed to one position when he left Jerusalem; according to the effect of his whole life he was irrevocably convinced of the supremacy of Christ when he reappeared in Jerusalem preaching the faith which he once destroyed. Some of this thinking may have taken place during the days of his blindness in Damascus; but if a period of several months' retirement in Arabia really took place, a much more adequate explanation is given for the tone of finality in his epistles, which show no uncertainty of conviction concerning the fundamental tenets of his personal faith. The main questions had been settled once for all.

The broad outline of the subsequent events as Galatians sketches them accords fairly well with the narrative of Acts. The visit to Jerusalem which took place after the three years in Damascus (1:18) should be equated with the appearance recorded in Acts 9:26-29. Most of the apostles had by this time left Jerusalem (Gal. 1:19, though Cephas and James, the Lord's brother, were still in the city. Acts states that Barnabas introduced Paul to the apostles, but does not name them.

There is no essential conflict between Galatians 1:19 and Acts 9:27, since the latter does not specify which apostles were present and which were absent. Paul's statement that he went into Syria and Cilicia after the return to Jerusalem agrees with Acts 9:30, which says that he departed for Tarsus, a city of Cilicia.

The stay in Jerusalem was brief but significant. It gave the leaders an opportunity to see for themselves the transformation of the erstwhile persecutor. At this time began his friendship with the Cypriote Jew, Barnabas, which later became so fruitful in the ministry in Antioch. Here also he encountered the antagonism of the Hellenistic Jews which pursued him all of his life, and which may be regarded as basic to the whole Galatian problem. Apparently he was not in Jerusalem long enough to make an impression on the Judean churches (Gal. 1:22), but he did receive the approbation of the apostles, and was generally befriended by the Jerusalem brethren.

Neither Luke nor Paul himself supplied any particulars of the years spent in Cilicia. Probably he made his headquarters at Tarsus; for that is where Barnabas found him when he invited him to take part in the ministry at Antioch (Acts 11:25, 26). He must have been engaged in preaching; for in Acts 15:41 Luke said that he "went through Syria and Cilicia, confirming the churches," though nowhere previously in Acts has the founding of these churches been mentioned. Paul's main purpose was not to narrate the details of his career, but simply to show that he had been active in proclaiming the message which he himself had believed.

The narrative in Galatians 2:1-10 is one of the historical puzzles of Paul's life. To what episode does it refer? In this biographical section he recounted only two visits to Jerusalem: the one which he made three years after his conversion, and this conference with James, Cephas, and John. In Acts three visits are recorded: (1) the return from Damascus shortly after his conversion, mentioned in Acts 9:26-30; (2) the "famine visit" of 11:27-30 and 12:25; and (3) the Council of Jerusalem which was held after the first missionary journey. The first of these can be equated with the early post-conversion visit as stated above. The real problem is whether the second visit of Galatians should be identified with the second or third visit of Acts.

If the second visit in Galatians is to be regarded as identical with the "famine visit," then Paul said nothing of the relief which the Antioch church was sending to the church in Jerusalem; and conversely, Luke omitted completely any reference to the question which, according to Galatians, was the real issue of the visit. Does Paul's declaration, "I went up by revelation" (2:2), accord with the statement in Acts that he and Barnabas were appointed by the church in Antioch as a relief committee? (Acts 11:29, 30) Furthermore, although the famine occurred "in the days of Claudius" (Acts 11:28) which extended from A.D. 41 to 54, Josephus stated more explicitly that there was a severe famine in Palestine between the years 44 and 48 in the procuratorships of Cuspius Fadus and Tiberius Alexander.[5]

If a median date for the famine be selected, Paul's "famine visit" probably took him to Jerusalem about A.D. 46.[6] According to the account in Galatians (1:18; 2:1), an interval of three years elapsed between Paul's conversion and his first visit to Jerusalem, and another interval of fourteen years came between the first visit and the interview with the apostles which is recorded in the second chapter. If, as seems most probable, these two interviews were successive, seventeen full years after his conversion would make A.D. 46 a bit early for the event of Galatians 2. Even by allowing that ancient methods of reckoning a fractional part of a year as a whole might

---

5. Josephus: *Antiquities*, iii, 15, 3; xx, 2, 5 and 5, 2. See also George H. Allen, "Procurator," in *International Standard Bible Encyclopaedia*, IV, 2457b, 2458.
6. Cf. Smith, *op. cit.*, pp. 646, 647.

reduce the time from seventeen to fifteen years, the conversion of Paul would have to be placed in A.D. 31, which scarcely gives time for the growth of the church depicted in the first seven chapters of Acts. This objection is not insuperable, for the events which transpired between Pentecost and the conversion of Paul may not have required more than two or three years. Acts gives little information as to exact dating of the crises in the apostolic church.

Because of the chronological difficulty involved in identifying the conference of Galatians 2:1-10 with the "famine visit" of Acts 11:29, 30, many expositors have chosen to make it the private aspect of the Council described in Acts 15:1-35.[7] Some factors seem to favor this view. The question discussed in the private interview, "the gospel which I preach among the Gentiles" (Gal. 2:2), presupposes that Paul had been exercising a ministry among Gentiles, which would accord with his preaching on the first journey through southern Galatia (Acts 13, 14). Furthermore, this "gospel" was closely related to the issue of circumcision which precipitated the Council. Galatians states that the interview was imperative because of "false brethren" (Gal. 2:4) who sought to bring the church into bondage. Acts shows that the Council was called because "certain men came down from Judea and taught the brethren, saying, Except ye be circumcised after the custom of Moses, ye cannot be saved" (Acts 15:1). James and Peter are mentioned both in Galatians 2 and in Acts 15, whereas in Acts 11 they are not mentioned at all, unless they might be included in the "elders" (Acts 11:30). The common conclusion is that Galatians affords insight into the private aspect of the Council, while Acts describes the public debates and the official action.

The chief objection to this identification of the second visit in Galatians with the Jerusalem Council is the evident inten-

---

7. Conybeare and Howson, *op. cit.,* pp. 821-828. See also Lightfoot, *op. cit.,* pp. 123-128.

tion of Paul to catalog all of his contacts with the Jerusalem church in order that he might prove to the satisfaction of the Galatians his independence of apostolic control. His statement in 1:20, "Now touching the things which I write unto you, behold, before God, I lie not," seems to imply that his list was complete to date. If the famine visit was not mentioned in Galatians, such a deliberate omission is hard to justify in the light of Paul's evident intent and emphasis. Furthermore, if the Council were intended in 2:1-10, why should Paul have said nothing about its decisions when they would be so pertinent to the situation which he was discussing?

Probably the controversy over this point will never be settled to the satisfaction of all concerned. Almost every inferential argument from one side can be matched by another inferential argument from the other side. For the sake of definiteness, the identity of the private conference in Galatians 2:1-10 with the "famine visit" will be conceded for the following reasons:

1. The chronology, though doubtful, is possible.

2. Paul's insistence that he had catalogued accurately his trips to Jerusalem would be worthless if he had deliberately omitted reference to the "famine visit."

3. The phrase "by revelation" (Gal. 2:2) may refer to the prophecy of Agabus (Acts 11:28), which was the motivating cause of the "famine visit."

4. The fact that there was a private conference calls for an occasion different from that of the Council, plans for which were discussed before the whole church at Antioch (Acts 15:2, 3). Why would Paul have sought a private hearing if the whole issue had already become a public controversy?

5. If Paul had already been conducting an extensive mission among the Gentiles, as recorded in Acts 13 and 14, his consultation with the apostles and his use of Titus as "Exhibit A" of the Gentile converts (Gal. 2:3) would be somewhat

belated. Such a situation would be merely discussing the advisability of what had already been accomplished.

6. The vacillation of Cephas at Antioch between the liberal attitude of eating with Gentile converts and withdrawing from their company when "certain came from James" (Gal. 2:11-14) is more understandable if it happened before the Council rather than after it. If no official decision concerning the status of Gentile converts had been announced, Cephas' uncertainty of action is explainable, whether it is excusable or not. The plain implication of "But when Cephas came to Antioch" (2:11) is that there had been an interview with Cephas somewhere else, and that he reversed his position on a later visit to Antioch.

7. On the basis of the private decision at the time of the "famine visit" (Gal. 2:6-10), Barnabas and Paul could have begun their mission. The public controversy of Acts 15 arose when their success became known and when the significance of its implications dawned upon the Judaizing group in the church at Jerusalem.

8. The attitude of Peter in Acts 15, where Luke quoted him as saying that the law is "a yoke upon the neck of the disciples which neither our fathers nor we were able to bear," can well be explained if Paul's colloquy with him in Galatians 2 preceded it. If Galatians 2 follows Acts 15 in order, Peter's attitude is quite difficult of explanation.[8]

9. According to the best chronological evidence,[9] the second and third visits to Jerusalem were not more than three or four years apart. The general controversy which had been raging

---

8. Cf. K. & S. Lake, *An Introduction to the New Testament* (New York: Harper and Bros., Publishers, 1937), pp. 81, 82. Lake attempts to solve the problem by making Acts 11:30 and Acts 15 two stories of one event which Luke treated as a continuous story. Such a solution is a *tour de force,* and does an injustice to Luke.
9. See Smith, *op. cit.,* pp. 646-648. Smith concurs in assigning Gal. 2:1-10 to the "famine visit." Cf. also Sir Wm. Ramsay, *St. Paul, the Traveller and the Roman Citizen* (New York: G. P. Putnam's Sons, 1909) pp. 51-60.

in the churches would only be increased by the reports of the widespread conversion of Gentiles that Paul brought back from his first journey into Galatia, since the Judaizing faction in the church would have known nothing of the private agreement between Paul and the leaders of the church at Jerusalem.

10. Either theory must account for some omission. Paul's failure to mention three visits to Jerusalem in his narrative can readily be explained if the Council of Jerusalem had not been held up to the time of the writing of Galatians. On the other hand, Luke's omission of the private conference from his account of the "famine visit" in Acts is attributable to the fact that he was chiefly interested in what the church and its leaders did publicly, not privately. He made no pretense of composing an exhaustive account of the inner workings of the apostolic church, while in Galatians Paul vehemently insisted that he was telling all that happened to date relative to the issue under discussion (Gal. 1:20).

If, however, the second visit of Galatians is equated with the Council, Paul's omission of the "famine visit" and Luke's omission of the private aspect of the Council must be explained in some other way. Why should Paul have deliberately overlooked the "famine visit" if he wanted to allay all suspicion concerning his connections with Judea? Why should Luke have failed to note the agreement between Paul and the "pillars" (Gal. 2:9) if that agreement had direct bearing upon the validity of the Gentiles' standing in the church? If ease of explanation is a fair criterion for a choice, the former alternative seems more plausible.

11. The time between the end of the first journey and the Council (Acts 14:28) was possibly long enough to admit of some correspondence with the Galatian churches; and the dissension in Antioch with the "certain men that came down from Judea" may coincide with the "certain . . . from James" mentioned in Galatians 2:12. Even should the argument with Cephas precede the first journey, the foregoing hypothesis fits the

conditions of the period preceding the Council better than it does those of the period following the Council.

The controversy with Cephas revealed two aspects of Paul's character: his willingness to accept responsible leadership in a time of controversy and uncertainty, and his personal detestation of any kind of compromise in action. It is noteworthy that Paul and not Barnabas took the lead in protesting Cephas' vacillation. Barnabas was a more amicable person than Paul, and in the case of John Mark (Acts 15:36-40) his confidence was ultimately justified. Paul, however, would rather make a clear decision on the merits of the moment than to risk the future of an important movement on the probability of change. His rebuke of Cephas shows his boldness and the consistency of his thinking. If this episode preceded the Council, it may mark the beginning of the breach between him and Barnabas which culminated in their separation afterwards. Perhaps Paul felt that Barnabas' judgment was as untrustworthy as John Mark's character.

Up to this point the biographical data have concerned chiefly the outward acts of Paul's life. The reported dialogue with Cephas, beginning in Galatians 2:14 verged into a monologue in which Paul laid before the Galatians the inward character of his faith. True biography must also take into account the undercurrents of mind and heart which are seldom openly declared, but which are the motivating forces behind the outward life. Galatians 2:19-21 may constitute the conclusion of what Paul said to Cephas, or may be his editorial message to the Galatians. In any case, it expressed the deepest experience of his life, from which all his theology flowed: "With Christ I stand crucified; I am no longer living, but in me lives Christ; and whatever life I am now living in the flesh, I am living by that faith which is characterized by the Son of God who loved me and gave himself in my stead." [10]

10. Original translation of Galatians 2:20.

The significance of this confession would demand a separate essay for adequate exposition. It is sufficient to point out here that Paul was referring to a climactic experience, now in the past,[11] which changed the current of his whole life, and which made the Christ a reality to him. Faith was for him not only the assumption of a historic fact, but was also a constant contact with a living person. This fundamental concept of faith is latent in the opening sentence of the epistle, "through Jesus Christ and God the Father, who raised him from the dead," and persists to the conclusion where he spoke of bearing in his body the brands of Jesus (6:17).

Scattering allusions of biographical worth may be found outside of the immediate section which has been discussed. In 3:1 Paul spoke of his style of preaching, suggesting that it was as vivid as if a placard had been hung before the eyes of the Galatians.[12] In 4:12-20 he mentioned his first visit. Evidently he had either been delayed among them by illness, or else he had been forced to leave his projected route to stay among them, for he says "Ye know that because of an infirmity of the flesh I preached the gospel unto you the first time" (4:13). The nature of the infirmity is not stated, but the figure of speech which follows in the next verses is taken by some to convey the idea that Paul had suffered from some sort of eye ailment. His use of "large letters" (6:11) has sometimes been employed as evidence that his sight was impaired; but it is more likely that he used the "large letters" for emphasis of his personal feelings. Whatever his illness may have been, it evoked the sympathy of the Galatians, who welcomed him "as an angel of God" (4:14). They did not regard him with contempt, although they might have been expected logically to

11. Greek: *sunestauromai*, "I stand crucified." The perfect tense refers not only to his present experience, but also to the past event that determined it.

12. Greek: *prographo*, "openly set forth." See J. H. Moulton & G. Milligan, *The Vocabulary of the Greek New Testament* (Grand Rapids, Mich., Wm. B. Eerdmans Publishing Company, 1949), p. 538.

do so. The ailment which is described so indefinitely here was probably the "thorn in the flesh" of II Corinthians 12 which proved so painful and so embarrassing to him in his ministry that he asked God to remove it. [13]

A curious reference appears in 5:11 where he said: "But I, brethren, if I still preach circumcision, why am I still persecuted?" It is obvious from the general representation in Galatians of the accusations against Paul that he had not been preaching circumcision. The Judaizers' objection to him was that he did not require it when they thought it should be obligatory. This quotation seemingly implies that he had preached circumcision, or at least that he believed that others thought he was preaching it. What possible ground would there have been for such an inference? If Galatians were written after the third journey, it is quite possible that the circumcision of Timothy would be known to the Galatian churches, and that some of them would accuse Paul of inconsistency. If Galatians were written earlier, the reference may indicate that he saw no obstacle to the circumcision of Jewish believers, but that he protested only the compulsory circumcision of Gentile converts. In any case, Paul adduced the persecution that he was suffering as evidence that he could not have changed his essential position on Gentile circumcision, or else the persecution would have ceased.

The Biographical Argument

Paul

The biographical data in Galatians were not written by Paul for the purpose of narrating interesting facts about himself but as a means of accounting for the stand which he took on the

---

13. Ramsay suggests in *A Historical Commentary on St. Paul's Epistle to the Galatians*, pp. 422-428, that Paul's sickness was an intermittent fever accompanied by headache. He rejects the hypothesis of epilepsy. For a fairly full discussion, see Hayes, *op. cit.*, pp. 38-46. Hayes favors the suggestion of acute ophthalmia.

relation of the law and the gospel. He wanted to show to the Galatians that his message was not a pose which he had adopted for the sake of expediency or from a desire for notoriety, but that it sprang from a divine intervention in his own life. His jealousy for his message was not bigotry, for in his anathema against those who perverted the gospel he included himself or the very angels from heaven if he or they should depart from revealed truth (Gal. 1:8). He was utterly convinced of the final truth of the gospel of Christ, and was ready to defend its verity and purity at all costs.

First of all, the autobiographical narrative indicates that he had not espoused the cause of the gospel because of any natural inclination toward it. All of his training and interest had been centered in the law, and there was no logical reason why he should abandon it. All of his family were under the law, his instructors had biased him in favor of the law, and he was advancing in its teachings with such rapidity that any sudden change of faith would be harmful to his scholastic prestige and to his social prominence in Jewry. He had absolutely nothing to gain, and much to lose by becoming a Christian.

Secondly, the sudden change of his faith was the direct result of divine intervention. Though Paul did not relate fully in Galatians the details of his conversion, his statement that "God . . . called me through his grace" (1:15) implied that he attributed his experience to God's objective act. He said that his gospel was given to him "through revelation of Jesus Christ" (1:12). A transcendent disclosure of a living Christ was made to his consciousness that gave him a completely new outlook on all of life.

Thirdly, his message was not taken over from new contacts or from a new environment. "Neither did I receive it from man, nor was I taught it," he declared (1:12). Upon his conversion he "conferred not with flesh and blood" (1:16). He did not immediately take counsel from the apostles in Jerusalem, who had been personally acquainted with Jesus and who could have told him much of Jesus' life and teaching; but he retired to Arabia where he was alone with his thoughts. Even when he did visit Jerusalem he saw only a few of the apostolic band, nor did he enter into contact with the churches of Judea where the gospel tradition was already established. Whatever message he had about Christ was formed when he began his public ministry and made his initial contacts with the original apostles.

Paul did not want his independence to be construed as heresy or as radical digression from the common core of apostolic teaching. After fourteen years of ministry he returned to Jerusalem in company with Barnabas, who had been his first sponsor among Christians after his conversion (Acts 9:27), and with Titus, who was one of the Gentile converts of his ministry (Gal. 2:3). The leading apostles, James, Cephas, and John were sufficiently impressed by Paul's account of himself and of his ministry to give to him and Barnabas the right hand of fellowship, and to recognize the difference in their ministries. Paul repudiated the suggestion that he was only an echo of the apostles, but he did make clear that he and they found themselves in fundamental agreement on the substance of their message, though they divided the field between them.

The apparent disagreement between Paul and the apostles arose over a question of consistency in behavior rather than in theology. Paul wanted to demonstrate to the Galatians that his conduct had been thoroughly consistent in his attitude on the Gentile question, whereas the attitude of the older apostles and leaders had not been consistent. If their stand had been quoted by the Judaizers as a pattern, it had been an irregular and an unreliable one, whereas Paul's stand for Gentile freedom had been the same throughout his ministry.

His position, then, was based on his own experience of Christ. With Christ he had died to the law, he had been united with Christ both in death and in life, and he had emerged into a living faith in the Son of God who justified sinners and who had entered into Paul's personal soul (Gal. 2:20). The autobiographical argument was calculated to show the historical validity of Paul's message as related to his own experience and to the experiential life of the Christianity of his day.

Other men than Paul are mentioned in Galatians, and their careers have some bearing on the interpretation of the book. No one of them is as much a part of the thought of Galatians as Paul; nevertheless they deserve some comment.

Cephas

Cephas was with Paul at Antioch at the time when the Gentile converts of the church were young in the faith and were susceptible of being easily swayed or influenced in almost any direction. Cephas had come to Antioch during Paul's ministry there which can be dated prior to A.D. 47. He was one of the leaders of the church in Jerusalem, and was undoubtedly identical with Peter.[14] His usual field of ministry was "unto

---

14. Cf. John 1:42: "Thou art Simon the son of John: thou shalt be called Cephas (which is by interpretation, Peter)." The relatively late date for the writing of the Fourth Gospel indicates that this title of Peter must have been still used in the church. Why his Aramaic name should have been used among Gentiles such as the Galatians, who probably knew him only by reputation, is not easily explicable. Perhaps Paul was still thinking in Aramaic terms if Galatians were written at an early date.

The identity of Cephas and Peter has been disputed by some scholars, who hold that Cephas was one of the early disciples, but not identical with Simon, Andrew's brother. K. Lake, in "Notes" published in the *Harvard Theological Review* XIV (1921), 95-97, commenting on Gal. 2:8, 9, says: "To call the same man by two names in the same sentence is, to say the least, a curious device, and Clement of Alexandria is quoted by Eusebius as believing that Cephas is intended to be different from Peter." Donald W. Riddle, "The Cephas-Peter Problem and a Possible Solution," *Journal of Biblical Literature*, 59 (1940), 169-180, suggests that there were among the early Christian leaders one whose name was Cephas and another whose name was Simon. Tradition pointed to Cephas as the person to whom Jesus first appeared after the resurrection. In the change from the use of Aramaic to Greek as the language of the early Christian church, the names of the two were artificially identified and the two were

the circumcision" (2:9), but he seems to have taken at Antioch a somewhat more liberal stand toward Gentiles than he would have taken at Jerusalem, since he ate with them (2:12). No orthodox Jew would ordinarily eat with Gentiles since their food was regarded as ceremonially unclean. With the recollection of his experience at the house of Cornelius, however, Peter probably felt that he was not transgressing the will of God by such action.

Peter's change of attitude was doubtless prompted by expediency rather than by conviction. When the strict Jewish brethren from Jerusalem came down to Antioch, he withdrew from the Gentiles, and separated from their company. The inconsistency of this act provoked Paul's ire. If Peter, as a Jew, were going to eat with the Gentiles on one occasion, why not on another? Least of all should he make a concession to the rigid party that insisted on circumcision for Gentiles; for by so doing he was eating with the Gentiles at one hour, and then tacitly agreeing in the next hour that the Gentiles should not enter into fellowship with him unless they became proselytes to Judaism before becoming valid Christians.

Such inconsistency was not alien to Peter's nature. At the last meeting in the upper room he had first refused to allow Jesus to wash his feet, and then, upon Jesus' remonstrance, had said: "Lord, not my feet only, but also my hands and my head" (John 13:9). He had boasted openly that he would never desert his Lord, and had been the first to deny Him (Luke 22:33, 34; 54-62; John 13:37, 38; 18:25-27). The action was quite in keeping with Peter's impetuous character.

Paul's treatment of Peter in Galatians is brief indeed; but he represented him as a leader in the church, and as an equal in the ministry of Christ. There is no indication of any perma-

accidentally confused.

These theories reject completely the historicity of John 1:42. G. LaPiana points out in *Harvard Theological Review* XIV (1921), 187-193 that "in the pre-Nicene Christian literature of the West there is no hint of the slightest doubt about the identity of Peter with the man who quarrelled with Paul at Antioch."

nent hostility between them, nor that either regarded the other as essentially inferior to himself. There seems to have been tacit agreement in the theological content of their messages. Paul's argument with Peter was not founded on any essential difference in their Christology nor upon any disagreement over the fact that Gentiles should be saved by faith. Paul protested only the irregularity of Peter's conduct, which was traceable chiefly to social pressure.

Barnabas

Barnabas is mentioned twice in Galatians as Paul's friend and associate. They were together in Jerusalem on the visit described in 2:1-10, and also at Antioch when Cephas came there (Gal. 2:13). Barnabas was one of the earliest converts in the church. He was a Jew of Cyprus, a Levite by descent, and a man of some wealth (Acts 4:36). Apparently he was one of those who had become believers about the time when Peter and John were active in Jerusalem, so that he had been associated with the disciples there from the days prior to the death of Herod. He possessed a warm and generous nature. He sacrificed his holdings in order that he might give to the poor (Acts 4:37), and jeopardized his reputation with the church by sponsoring Saul of Tarsus shortly after his conversion when he was still regarded as an enemy of the Christians (Acts 9:27). Barnabas, more than any other man had been responsible for the development of the Gentile church at Antioch, and had been the means of drawing Paul into that enterprise (Acts 11:22, 25, 26). The two had worked together quite amicably, and had succeeded in building a strong church. It had inaugurated a program of relief for the persecuted and impoverished church in Jerusalem.

In Galatians 2:13 Paul indicated that Barnabas did not act quite consistently in the crisis which took place at Antioch. Barnabas' action, however, was understandable if not excusable. He had been sent to Antioch by the church of Jerusalem and he had tried to maintain friendly relationships with it. He had carried relief to its poor, and had contributed to its needs himself. If then its delegates came down to Antioch, he wanted to spare their feelings as much as possible by not flaunting the Gentile liberty in their faces; and so he withdrew from Gentile fellowship while they were in the city. Paul's implied censure of Barnabas (2:13, 14) was doubtless justified; but one wonders whether Paul had understood fully Barnabas' motives, and whether the breach that finally separated them may not have begun at this point.

The account in Galatians does not state whether this episode in Antioch occurred before or after the first missionary journey; in fact, Galatians does not mention the missionary journeys directly at all. In all probability the disagreement took place after the first preaching tour in Asia Minor; for Paul's interest in the Gentiles and his prestige in the apostolic circles were probably effects of this ministry. The defection of Peter and Barnabas, however, seems to have been only temporary; for both took the side of Gentile liberty at the Council of Jerusalem (Acts 15:7,12), and agreed with Paul in his contentions. Upon the agreement of the Council that the Gentiles should be exempted from certain requirements of the law, Barnabas was delighted to accompany Paul in reporting to the churches the results of the Council (Acts 15:25), and in the discharge of this mission he spent further time with Paul in the church at Antioch (Acts 15:35).

Paul's proposal to revisit the churches which had been founded on the first journey precipitated a crisis. Barnabas "was minded"[15] to take his relative Mark with them. Paul stubbornly insisted that he should not go, because he had failed them on the first journey. In a sense, both were right. The importance and danger of the mission made inadvisable the inclusion of a man of such a doubtful record as Mark's. On the

---

15. Greek *ebouleto.* Imperfect tense, indicating current intention.

other hand, Barnabas probably understood Mark better than Paul, and had estimated correctly that his repentance was genuine. The disagreement was settled by separation. Paul went back to Asia Minor, and Barnabas went to Cyprus. From this point on, Barnabas disappeared from the narrative of Acts (Acts 15:39, 40). The reference to Barnabas in I Corinthians 9:6, written at a later period in Paul's career, indicates that he knew that Barnabas was still preaching, and that they were still on friendly terms.

James

The James who is mentioned in Galatians (2:9, 12) was undoubtedly the brother of the Lord who became leader of the church in Jerusalem after Peter's miraculous release from imprisonment and subsequent departure from the city (Acts 12:17b). James the brother of John and son of Zebedee had been put to death by Herod at approximately the same time that Paul and Barnabas went up to Jerusalem on the "famine visit" (Acts 12:1, 2). Since a James was present at the Council of Jerusalem, which took place several years later than the "famine visit," he must have been the second James, the Lord's brother, whose influence was strong in Jerusalem. Evidently he was inclined to a strict interpretation of the law, for both at the Council of Jerusalem (Acts 15:13ff.) and Paul's visit to Jerusalem ten years later after the completion of his third journey (Acts 21:18-26) this man was a defender of the Jewish-Christian position which combined faith in Christ with zeal for the law.

The allusion in Galatians 2:12 confirms the implication of Acts that James was the leader of the circumcision party in Jerusalem. James may not have been directly responsible for the Judaizing party in Galatia. Possibly they had exaggerated his attitude into a legalism and into a hostility to Paul that James himself would not have countenanced. He was, however, the model for the Judaizer; and the scrutiny of those who "came from James" prompted Peter's sudden change in attitude at Antioch.

There was, then, in the early church, a difference of emphasis among the leaders themselves. This difference did not become a break of unity, for James himself proposed the ruling in the Jerusalem Council that freed the Gentiles from observance of the full ceremonial law, and his proposal was acceptable to Paul and Barnabas. It is possible that men who possessed James' viewpoint without his discretion produced the tension at Antioch described in Galatians, and that they were the agitators whose activity created the necessity for the Council (Acts 15:1,2).

Titus

Titus, who later became one of Paul's associates in his itinerant ministry, is introduced here (Gal. 2:1, 3). He was a Gentile, probably one of the early converts at Antioch, who was selected as a prize example of the possibility of salvation apart from the law. If Galatians 2:1 be equated with the "famine visit," Titus must have been an active worker in the church at Antioch not later than A.D. 46. If this be true, it would be interesting to know why Paul and Barnabas did not take Titus with them on their first missionary journey instead of John Mark, whom they imported specially from Jerusalem (Acts 12:25). Was it because they felt that the tension between Jewish and Gentile Christians was such that a Gentile assistant would widen a breach already existing? And did Mark's subsequent unwillingness to accompany Paul and Barnabas into the highlands of Asia Minor, where the population was largely Gentile, indicate that John Mark was unwilling to engage too deeply in Gentile work? Did Titus' later prominence at Corinth during the third journey show that Paul made him a worker among Gentile churches who could deal with them more effectively than Paul could himself? (II Cor. 7:6, 14; 8:6, 16, 23). Perhaps Titus' early experience with the situation at Antioch enabled him to deal more vigorously with ecclesiastical disagreements which involved this issue in Gentile churches.

John

The last person mentioned in Galatians is John. No important action is assigned to him in the only place where his name occurs (2:9). Doubtless he was identical with John the son of Zebedee, since no other John was among the leaders of the church of Jerusalem at that time.

The strong biographical emphasis of Galatians shows that the book was not written from an impersonal theoretical viewpoint. It was connected directly with practical problems of the apostolic age which involved the lives of actual people. Because its principles were thus illustrated in the personal conduct of living men, and because human nature does not change radically through the centuries, the book still possesses a warm and persuasive message for people of the modern world. The truths for which Paul stood were vitally related to the life of his day, and insofar as men are the same now, these truths are still relevant.

THE HISTORICAL SETTING

The Historical Method

CHAPTER IV

THE HISTORICAL SETTING

The Historical Method

THE INTERPRETATION of any piece of literature like Galatians depends upon its relation to its historical background. Allusions to contemporary events, to places, to trends and movements, and to questions of the day in which it was written must always be explained in order to illumine clearly the thought of the writing. Only as the teaching of any book is seen in the larger context of the situation that produced it can a true perspective on its meaning be obtained.

Although Galatians does not carry any direct statement concerning its date and destination beyond the somewhat ambiguous reference to the churches of Galatia (Gal. 1:2), it was obviously sent to a certain group of people who were localized in space and time, and it was produced in a definite period of Paul's ministry. Considerable discussion has already been devoted to these questions in the foregoing chapters on the critical and biographical methods; consequently the purpose of this chapter will center on the place of Galatians in the thinking of Paul and of the early church rather than on the chronological and topographical details connected with the book.

The Setting in Paul's Ministry

The place of Galatians in Paul's ministry can be determined with some accuracy. Since the events recounted in the biographical section were already in the past, the letter must have been written after the founding of the churches of Galatia, and

after the visit of Paul and Barnabas to Jerusalem, following
their initial ministry in Antioch. Paul's allusion to "the gospel which I preach among the Gentiles" (Gal. 2:2) could refer to his preaching in Cilicia and in Antioch, both of which
preceded the first missionary journey (Acts 9:30; 11:25, 26).
On the basis of the early date for Galatians (A.D. 48), the
book will fit in the beginning of Paul's missionary career,
prior to the separation between him and Barnabas (Acts 15:
39, 40). This dating would make Galatians contemporane-
ous with the struggle against the Judaizers which came to a
crisis in the Council of Jerusalem, and which did not subside
entirely until some years later.

On the other hand, if, as some hold, the reference to his
"former" visit (4:13) implied that he visited Galatia on two
separate occasions, then the epistle can hardly have been written prior to the middle of his second journey. His evident
surprise at the rapid defection of the Galatian Christians
(1:6) shows that the situation was unanticipated, and that it
must have come upon him without any previous warning. In
making his reply to this defection, he did not quote precedents
taken from experience in other localities, which might indicate that he had not worked in many other places before he
learned of their failure. In any case, the book was written in
the period when Paul was waging a theological warfare with
a Judaism which was militantly opposed to the preaching of
Jesus as the Messiah. In almost every city which Paul visited
on this second journey after leaving Galatia — Philippi, Thes-
salonica, Beroea, Athens, Corinth — the conflict with Judaism
is mentioned. Obviously Paul was not insisting that the Gentiles should submit to circumcision and keep all the law. Were
he doing so, the Hellenistic Jews of these Greek cities to which
he went would welcome him as an aid to their proselyting activities. Galatians was written in the midst of persecution
(5:11), and so might fit into the early half of the second jour-

ney as well as into the period just before the Council at Jerusalem.

Still another view places the composition of Galatians in Paul's third journey, possibly in Ephesus after his last visit to the Galatian country. There is less likelihood of this possibility, as has been shown previously,[1] because the events described in the historical section of Galatians seem too fresh in his memory to allow for the writing of the book at a later period. The silence of Galatians concerning the activities in the church after A.D. 50 militates against a late date for the book, though the argument from silence cannot be conclusive.

Though absolute certainty of the date of Galatians may be unattainable, the likelihood that it belongs to the earlier rather than to the later ministry of Paul seems more probable. What inferences can be drawn from this probability?

First, Galatians was the product of a controversy over the nature of the Christian message which Paul himself had not sought, but which was unavoidable. The preaching of truth always produces disagreement with those who reject it. Jesus was frequently engaged in argument with the rulers of His nation who did not accept His message. Although the church in Jerusalem was chiefly Jewish, its emphasis upon the resurrection of Jesus and His exaltation to the right hand of God involved it in conflict with Judaism. The conversion of Paul alienated him immediately from those who had been his colleagues in Judaism, and caused them to view with suspicion everything that he did and said, even to the point of violent opposition to his person and teachings. Furthermore, the Judaizing element within the church who wished to acknowledge Jesus of Nazareth as the Messiah and at the same time to maintain the full claims of the law confronted him with their propaganda. To their way of thinking, Paul was preaching only a partial Gospel, salvation without commandments and ceremonies, Christ without Moses. Because of this long

---

1. *Supra.* pp. 63, 64.

heritage of controversy, Paul was forced by circumstances to define his position since he had been engaged from the first in a ministry to Gentiles. Galatians is the official statement of that position.

Secondly, if Galatians was written relatively early in Paul's career, it shows that his theology was not the product of a long evolution from Judaism fostered by Hellenistic influence, but that it was formulated quickly, and that its essential details were fixed at the outset of his ministry. There is no hint in the language of the introductory chapters that Paul had ever preached any other message than the one that Galatians contains, or that up to the time of writing he had planned to change his message. The theology of grace was clearly defined and firmly fixed in Paul's convictions from the outset of his career.

Thirdly, Galatians springs from the conflicts of an active ministry. Paul was not an armchair theologian. His convictions were hammered out on the anvil of intellectual struggle and of soul-suffering. Every line in this epistle is vibrant with the passion of a thinker to whom Christ is not only his ideal, but his life (Gal. 2:20). Paul reasoned by concrete analogy to the current formulas of his day, and when he did use logic, it was connected with the actual needs of daily life, and was not formulated in a vacuum. Galatians still carries the acrid odor of the arena, and not the lingering mustiness of some ivory tower of intellectual detachment.

The History of the Galatian Church

The Galatian churches were the firstfruits of Paul's leadership in the church's ministry to the Gentiles. Prior to his connection with Barnabas in the work at Antioch he had been engaged in an independent ministry in Syria and Cilicia (Acts 9:30; 11:25; Gal. 1:21). When he and Barnabas were sent out by the Antiochian church on the first evangelistic mission, they began in Cyprus, which was Barnabas' home territory

(Acts 4:36), and they were known there as Barnabas and Saul. When they left Cyprus for the mainland of Asia Minor, Luke referred to them as "Paul and his company" (Acts 13: 13). If the change in phraseology means anything, it indicates that Paul as the younger and more aggressive man had assumed the leadership, and that henceforth the mission was his rather than that of Barnabas.

The mission under Paul began with the preaching in the synagogue of Antioch of Pisidia. The sermon which is given in Acts 13:16-43 is the first recorded address of Paul in Acts. Luke evidently regarded it as a keynote speech, setting the precedent for Paul's later message and ministry. There are several elements in it which are relevant to the interpretation of the Galatian situation.

1. The address was thoroughly Jewish in approach. It consisted mainly of a review of God's dealings with Israel, emphasizing His gift to them of leaders: Saul, as the first king, then David, and finally in fulfilment of the promises made to David, Jesus, whom the nation had rejected. The appeal to the Messianic hope was presented first.

2. The significance of the resurrection was stressed. On the basis of historic fact confirmed by witness (Acts 13:30), on the basis of the promise given to the fathers (Acts 13:32), and on the basis of predictive prophecy (Acts 13:33), the resurrection was made the foundation of faith. Paul applied this truth personally in Galatians 2:20: "Christ liveth in me."

3. The address drew a clear distinction between justification by faith and justification by works. "Through this man is proclaimed unto you remission of sins: and by him every one that believeth is justified from all things, from which ye could not be justified by the law of Moses" (Acts 13:38, 39). This statement is the core of the entire Pauline message, and is the center of argument in the Galatian epistle.

4. Paul boldly asserted that the Gentiles were to be saved by faith in his message. The words "Every one that believeth"

in 13:39 would certainly include both Jew and Gentile in their scope, and the later declaration of Paul and Barnabas confirms the inference: "Seeing ye thrust it from you, and judge yourselves unworthy of eternal life, lo, we turn to the Gentiles" (Acts 13:46). The Gentile hearers understood that the message was intended for them, and they believed (Acts 13:48).

The first stage of preaching in the South Galatian territory was thus marked (1) by an initial appeal to the Jews and proselytes through contact with the synagogue, (2) by the rise of Jewish opposition to the new message, and (3) by the beginning of a distinctively Gentile mission which was enthusiastically welcomed by the Gentiles.

The second stage of the mission developed in Lystra. There the approach was totally different because apparently there was no synagogue. The Jewish population of the city must have been small. The initial address was made in the public square as an outcome of a miracle of healing. When the Gentile pagans undertook to offer a sacrifice to Paul and Barnabas, whom they regarded as gods, the latter protested vehemently. They presented "a living God, who made the heaven and the earth and the sea, and all that in them is" (Acts 14:15). Their concept of God was that of the Old Testament revelation, but their presentation of Him was in terms that the Gentiles would understand — the Creator and Sustainer of men, who "did good and gave you from heaven rains and fruitful seasons, filling your hearts with food and gladness" (Acts 14:17).

Jewish opposition appeared again, and so aroused the prejudice of the Gentiles that they stoned Paul out of the city. Nevertheless, he and Barnabas "made many disciples" (Acts 14:21) in Derbe, and upon returning through Lystra, Iconium, and Pisidian Antioch, they organized churches by appointing elders in each one (Acts 14:23).

The initial mission, then, seemed to be a success. There had been genuine and eager belief among the Gentiles in spite of Jewish opposition; a chain of churches had been organized in new territory; and the effectiveness of salvation by faith upon those of non-Jewish background seemed to be demonstrated incontrovertibly.

The importance of this mission to the history of the early church in general is indicated by the amount of space that Luke assigned to it in the book of Acts. Obviously he did not pretend to record everything that took place between A.D. 30 and A.D. 60, for his omissions are quite as conspicuous as his inclusions. Nothing is said, for instance, of Paul's mission in Tarsus and Cilicia before his call to Antioch, although he labored in those regions for almost a decade, and perhaps longer. Not a hint is given of what the twelve apostles were doing in this period, though they were probably in Jerusalem (8:1) for a part of the time, nor is the reader told where they went when they finally left the city. The fact that Luke described this mission as fully as he did shows that he attached some importance to it.

Did Luke treat this mission in detail because the controversy which was begun between the Jews and Paul before the founding of the Gentile church in this territory was perpetuated within the church after its establishment? Does the "and" which begins Acts 15 indicate that in Luke's presentation the Council of Jerusalem was not just one more episode in the development of the church, but that it had a very close connection with the trends of chapter 14? Was the dispute over circumcision which began at Antioch and which resulted in the Council simply the full outcome of a tendency first manifested in Galatia? If so, the background of the Galatian letter becomes all the clearer; for one can then see in it the preliminary struggle which Paul waged against the Judaizers in Galatia and against the irresolute leaders at Antioch before the final settlement was made in the Council.

At the Council, as described in Acts, certain topics were discussed which seem relevant to the development of the Galatian church. Enroute to the Council from Antioch through Phoenicia and Samaria, Paul and Barnabas were engaged in "declaring the conversion of the Gentiles" (Acts 15:3). A fair inference from this statement would be that the churches of this territory were largely Jewish in constituency, and that they had not previously been acquainted with the new missionary movement in which the Gentiles were being saved. The issue was joined in Jerusalem when the Pharisaic party in the church insisted, like the Galatian Judaizers, that the Gentile converts should be circumcised and that they should obey the Mosaic law (Acts 15:5). The speakers in the Council followed the order of the argument of Galatians. Peter's speech involved the biographical argument, for he cited his own experience in his opening words: "Brethren, ye know that a good while ago God made choice among you, that by my mouth the Gentiles should hear the word of the gospel, and believe" (Acts 15:7). He continued with a theological argument as he said: "And God . . . bare them witness, giving them the Holy Spirit, even as he did unto us, and he made no distinction between us and them, cleansing their hearts by faith . . . But we believe that we shall be saved through the grace of the Lord Jesus, in like manner as they" (Acts 15:8, 9, 11). The practical argument also is interjected, since he asked the searching question: "Now therefore why make ye trial of God, that ye should put a yoke upon the neck of the disciples which neither our fathers nor we were able to bear?" (Acts 15:10). The structure of Peter's speech makes one wonder whether it were not at least partially the result of Paul's argument with him at Antioch. If Paul said then to Peter what he wrote to the Galatian churches, it is easier to understand Peter's strong defense of Gentile liberty at the Council by a speech which resembles Galatians both in general content and structure.

The letter of James which summarized the results of the Council contained three statements that had a bearing on the later status of the Galatian churches. First, there was a public repudiation of the teachers who had claimed James as their authority for Judaizing activities. Paul, in Galatians 2:12, said flatly that Peter's defection at Antioch was occasioned by "certain [who] came from James." Perhaps he did blame James for their attitude. James' pronouncement at the Council, however, removed any ground for further objections or fears on Paul's part. Second, the letter of the Jerusalem church commended Barnabas and Paul officially (Acts 15:25), as well as Judas and Silas who returned with them to Antioch. In this way Paul's claim to the Galatians of approval by the "pillars" of the church (Gal. 2:9) was vindicated. Last of all, the restrictions placed upon the Gentile Christians were not intended as ceremonial adjuncts to saving faith, but merely as a means for removing obstacles to fellowship by avoiding needless offense to Jewish brethren. Paul himself, while defending the right of the Gentile Christian to freedom from ceremonial observance as a religious ritual, declared that "if meat causeth my brother to stumble, I will eat no flesh for evermore, that I cause not my brother to stumble" (I Cor. 8:13). There is, therefore, no contradiction between these decrees and the substance of Galatians; on the contrary, they simply enforced the principle given in Galatians that liberty should be tempered by comity.

The outcome of the Council was thus important for the Gentile churches of which the Galatian churches were the earliest. The second mission to these churches is recorded in Acts 16, where Luke stated that "as they [Paul and Silas] went on their way through the cities, they delivered them the decrees to keep which had been ordained of the apostles and elders that were at Jerusalem" (Acts 16:4). Not only were the churches of Derbe, Lystra, and Iconium mentioned by name, but apparently others were included which may not have been mentioned by Luke, or he may have referred to the churches of Syria and Cilicia (Acts 15:41). In any case, the decrees were publicized through the churches outside of Antioch which had been established up to this time, and they were regarded as expressing the final decision on the question of circumcision versus uncircumcision for Gentiles. Very little is said concerning the ultimate fate of the Galatian churches. Timothy was a product of Lystra, the son of one of Paul's converts of the first journey (Acts 16:2). He must have shared Paul's ministry there, for an allusion in II Timothy 3:10, 11 shows that their acquaintance at Lystra had been more than casual. The mention of the work of Galatia and Phrygia in Acts 18:23 implies dealing with individuals rather than with organized groups. There is no way of telling what the outcome of the Galatian controversy may have been, though probably the church responded to Paul's letter and mission by reaffirming its faith and liberty in Christ.

The Chronology of Galatians

Since the chronology of Galatians has already been discussed under the critical and biographical interpretation of the book, a brief summary will suffice.[2] Unlike the Gospel of Luke, which gives a definite dating for the beginning of its main narrative (Luke 3:1), the book of Galatians contains no fixed point of chronological reference, and the numerical periods of time which are given may be either successive or overlapping. The nearest approach to a *terminus a quo* for the chronology is the conversion of Paul, to which there seems to be a definite allusion in 1:15, 16:

> *But when it was the good pleasure of God, who separated me, even from my mother's womb, and called me through his grace, to reveal his Son in me, that I might preach him among the Gentiles; straightway I conferred not with flesh and blood . . .*

Since Acts 9:20 states that, after his conversion, "straightway in the synagogues, he [Paul] proclaimed Jesus, that he is the Son of God," the coincidence of the idea of immediate action in both of these passages may indicate that they refer to the

---

2. *Supra,* pp. 58-63 and 75-82.

identical event. This identification gives a starting point in
Paul's career for the events of Galatians, but does not afford
an exact dating for them, because the year of Paul's conversion is not known with certainty. On the assumption that it
took place within three years of Pentecost, it may be placed
tentatively about A.D. 31.[3] If so, the chronology of Galatians
may be charted as follows:

Event	Ref.	Time	
Conversion of Paul	1:15	A. D. 31	
Visit to Arabia	1:17		3 years
Return to Damascus			
First Visit to Jerusalem	1:18	33	
Interview with Cephas			
Spent 15 days in city			
Departure to Syria and Cilicia	1:21		14 years
(Early ministry in Antioch — not mentioned in Galatians)			
Second Visit to Jerusalem	2:1-10	46	
Accompanied by Barnabas and Titus			
Motivated by revelation			
Private interview			
Complaint about "false brethren"			
Agreement with James, Cephas, and John			No interval stipulated
(First Missionary Journey — not mentioned in Galatians. Implied by Pauline leadership in chapter 2)			
Visit of Cephas to Antioch, and resulting controversy	2:11ff.	48 (?)	
Writing of Galatians			
(Council of Jerusalem — not mentioned in Galatians)		48/49	

3. A. D. 31 may be early; but D. Smith, *Our Lord's Earthly Life* (New
York: George H. Doran, n.d.), pp. xi-xv, fixes the date of the crucifixion
at A. D. 29, which would make the foregoing dating possible.

The chronology as charted above allows for the overlapping of one year on the assumption that, according to common practice in Jewish chronology, a fraction of a year would be reckoned as a whole year.[4] If Paul were converted in A.D. 31, his return to Jerusalem would have occurred in A.D. 33, and by starting the second period of fourteen years in the same year, the last year would fall in A.D. 46. Such an interpretation will allow for the identification of the second visit to Jerusalem with the "famine visit" of Acts 11:28, 29, and also for the allotment of two years' time to the first missionary journey before the return to Antioch and the Council of Jerusalem. If Paul's conversion were in A.D. 32 or 33, the entire scale would be shifted accordingly. The Council, however, could not have been later than A.D. 50.

One thing is certain: Paul's argument from the sequence of historical events terminated with the story of the dispute at Antioch. Whether this occurred before the Council of Jerusalem or immediately afterward, the course of events in the church of Antioch which is treated as relevant to the situation of the Galatians is not traced beyond A.D. 50. Paul did not feel that he needed to discuss all the events of that period, but the fact that he made no mention of anything later might mean that Galatians was written not long after the critical years in which his status in this church and his mission were at stake. After A.D. 50 the trends in the church crystallized into policies which separated the Jewish and Gentile groups and which culminated in the practical disappearance of the former group with the destruction of Jerusalem in A.D. 70.

The Historical Importance of Galatians

Galatians is one of the most important historical documents that have survived from the apostolic age. It is the monument of a controversy which rocked the church, and which

4. Cf. Conybeare & Howson, *op. cit.*, Note B on p. 835.

ended in the achievement of complete liberty of conscience and faith for the Gentile converts. It marks the transition between a Christianity which was regarded by many as a sect of the Jews [5] and a Christianity which ultimately emerged as the independent faith of Gentiles and Jews alike. As the record of this transition, it has been a permanent check to formalism and legalism in the existing church, and has preserved the positive teaching on the meaning of salvation through faith in Christ.

Its historical value, however, is not solely in being the memento of a forgotten controversy. Had this epistle not been written, the whole face of Christianity might have been different, if, indeed, Christianity would have survived at all. Paul's championship of spontaneous faith versus entrenched legalism delivered the gospel from the trammels of Judaism, and set it free. Galatians became the permanent affirmation of the right of each individual to base his spiritual hope upon a direct personal relationship with Christ, plus nothing. Paul's personal confession in Galatians 2:20 has long been regarded as an epitome of the genius of the Christian life.

If Galatians was written before the Council of Jerusalem, it is the first of Paul's extant epistles, and is thus a witness to the early crystallization of his theological teaching. It shows that within twenty years of the death of Jesus the doctrine of justification by faith in Him was preached widely, and that it was the accepted message of the apostolic church. Even if it was written later in Paul's life, it carried the "historic faith" back to the very origins of the church, and demonstrated that it was not the product of an evolutionary process which took place long after the death of Jesus and of the apostles. The essence of Christian faith was discussed critically by the apostles at Jerusalem and in the meeting at Antioch before it was ever committed to paper. Galatians is thus a substantial guaranty of the purity of our theological heritage.

---

5. Acts 24 5. 14.

THE THEOLOGICAL FRAMEWORK

THE THEOLOGICAL METHOD

CHAPTER V

THE THEOLOGICAL FRAMEWORK

THE THEOLOGICAL METHOD

A LTHOUGH the books of the Bible are not primarily theological textbooks, they are replete with doctrinal content. Not only do they contain many sections where doctrine is directly and systematically discussed, but a great deal of teaching is implied in the action or in the presuppositions of the text. Sometimes the implied teaching is more important than what is expressed. The epistles of Paul, with the possible exception of Romans and Ephesians, were directed toward settling questions arising from emergencies in the churches rather than toward a systematic presentation of the entire range of Christian theology. One might question whether any such systematic presentation existed in the early church, were there not occasional allusions to a definite body of teaching which Paul possessed and which he imparted carefully to his converts (I Cor. 4:14-17, II Thess. 3:6).

The essential nature of this teaching lay in the declaration of I Corinthians 15:1-5:

> *Now I make known unto you, brethren, the gospel which I preached unto you, which also ye received, wherein also ye stand, by which also ye are saved, if ye hold fast the word which I preached unto you, except ye believed in vain. For I delivered unto you first of all that which also I received: that Christ died for our sins according to the scriptures; and that he was buried; and that he hath been raised on the third day according to the scriptures; and that he appeared to Cephas . . .*

The core of the Christian gospel as presented by Paul was the historic revelation of God in the person of Christ, who died for our sins and rose again; and in whom we find both the dynamic and pattern for an experience of eternal life. The varied inferences to be drawn from this central truth and the various applications of it to daily life were evoked by spiritual needs of the individual churches, and were recorded in the epistles which he sent to those churches in response to the crises that confronted them.

These central truths appear in every book of the New Testament even though they are not treated in patently systematic fashion. A careful canvass of the phraseology of any single book will often give a wide cross-section of the main premises which underlie its peculiar teaching. The process of searching through a book of the Bible to collate and to compare its doctrinal assumptions and statements is called the theological method.

There are three aspects of the theological method that may be pursued in the study of any book of the Bible: (1) the endeavor to define the assumptions that underlie the teaching of the book; (2) the topical codification of the explicit teachings which are prominent in the text; and (3) the separate treatment of any section of the book that may be predominantly theological in character. The application of the teaching thus discovered is the final task of the expositor.

The Theological Assumptions of Galatians

A representative treatment of one of the theological assumptions in Galatians appears in the following summary of its doctrine of God. Nowhere in the book is God defined metaphysically, nor is any proof offered for His existence; yet without the assumption of the existence of God and of His personal relation to men the entire book would be pointless. The actuality of God is simply taken for granted as one would take for granted his own existence; and the qualities of His being are implied in the language used. The references to God are more than two dozen in number, and are charted as follows:

NO.	REF.	TEXT
1	1:1	God the Father, who raised him [Christ] from the dead
2	1:3	God the Father
3	1:4	our God and Father
4	1:10	seeking the favor . . . of God
5	1:13	the church of God
6	1:15	the good pleasure of God
7	1:20	before God, I lie not
8	2:6	God accepteth not man's person
9	2:19	. . . live unto God
10	2:20	Son of God
11	2:21	the grace of God
12	3:6	Abraham believed God
13	3:8	God would justify the Gentiles
14	3:11	justified . . . before God
15	3:17	A covenant confirmed beforehand by God
16	3:18	God granted it by promise
17	3:20	God is one
18	3:21	. . . the promises of God
19	3:26	. . . sons of God
20	4:4	God sent forth His Son
21	4:6	God sent forth the Spirit
22	4:7	heir through God
23	4:8	not knowing God
24	4:9	know God
25	4:9	known by God
26	4:14	as an angel of God
27	5:21	the Kingdom of God
28	6:7	God is not mocked
29	6:16	Israel of God

The foregoing chart contains a complete list of the uses of the term "God" in Galatians, except for the expression "God forbid" in 2:17 and 3:21, where the word "God" does not occur in the Greek text. A survey of these passages will reveal certain facts:

1. The distribution of these allusions is confined largely to the first four chapters of Galatians. In the section of the book which deals with the practical application of its doctrine, God is scarcely mentioned.

2. The personal aspect of God is defined in the term "Father," which occurs three times. Once it describes the relation of God to Christ, and twice it describes His relation to men.

3. The sovereignty of God is assumed. The favor of God is the highest good (1:10); God is the ultimate standard of truth (1:20); He is infallible in His judgments (6:7); He initiates the salvation of men (3:8, 17, 18) by sending His Son and His Spirit to them (4:4, 6).

4. A personal relationship with God is possible (2:19; 4:9) and the justified man may enter into it (3:26; 4:7). The method and meaning of the justification on which this relationship is founded constitutes the main topic of theological discussion in Galatians.

5. This personal relationship with God is expressed in terms of sonship. God is introduced as Father (1:1,4); believers are declared to be sons of God through faith in Christ (3:26) who redeemed them that they might enter into that sonship (4:5). The consciousness of this sonship is created by the Holy Spirit, who prompts men to acknowledge God as Father (4:6).

From the foregoing implications two conclusions may be drawn. First, Galatians does not attempt an explicit and exhaustive treatment of the subject of God. Much more is assumed than is stated. Second, the incidental teaching on the subject of God is symmetrical rather than one-sided, and is directed toward the satisfaction of personal needs. Enough is taught about God, even casually, to acquaint a person with Him and to reveal His true nature.

Explicit Doctrinal Teaching

One doctrine that is taught directly and explicitly in this epistle is justification by faith as contrasted with salvation by

works. The word "justify" is used eight times in the text.
The usages may be charted as follows:

NO.	REF.	CONTENT
1	2:16	man is not *justified* by the works of the law
2	2:16	. . . we might be *justified* by faith in Christ
3	2:16	because "by the works of the law shall no flesh be justified" [Quotation from Ps. 143:2(?)]
4	2:17	. . . we sought to be *justified* in Christ . . .
5	3:8	. . . foreseeing that God would *justify* the Gentiles by faith
6	3:11	now that no man is *justified* by the law before God, is evident
7	3:24	. . . that we might be *justified* by faith
8	5:4	. . . ye who would be *justified* by the law

The instances given in the chart fall roughly into three groups. The first group are all centered about Galatians 2:16, 17, where the central thought of the book is announced in conjunction with the biographical argument which opens its discussion. The second group, 3:8, 11, 24, occur in the passage which presents the central thought of the book in an argumentative form. The last instance is part of the conclusion which Paul pressed on his readers both personally and practically. The doctrine is, therefore, related to each section of the epistle, and is a part of its central message.

The word itself [1] means to declare righteous, rather than primarily to be righteous or to make righteous. It was used in the current idiom to mean to judge rightly, to think right, to estimate correctly. As a legal term it meant to vindicate, which is its general use in the New Testament as stated above, to do justice to a person, and hence, occasionally, to punish, or to execute a sentence. In the New Testament it occurs outside of the writings of Luke and Paul only in the books of Matthew and of James. The two occurrences in Matthew (11:

1. Greek: *dikaioo*. For a discussion of the usage in the papyri, see Moulton & Milligan, *op. cit., in loco.*

19; 12:37) do not carry any theological connotation, and from the standpoint of doctrinal material may be considered as negligible. Three times in James, however (2:21, 24, 25), the term is used definitely with reference to the doctrine of justification, and seemingly with a resultant meaning quite opposite to that of Paul. Neither in Matthew nor in James is the essential meaning of *dikaioo* different from that which it bears in the Lukan and Pauline context.

In Luke and in Paul, with some few exceptions, *dikaioo* refers to the legal relation of the regenerate man to God. Whereas he was previously liable to judgment because he was a transgressor of God's commandments, and consequently condemned by law and conscience alike, through the death of Christ the way has been provided by which he has been given a new standing with God. He is declared legally righteous because he is given the standing of Christ, who suffered in his place. The claims of the law are satisfied, and the sinner is released from his guilt and from the penalty accompanying it.

To return to the passages in Galatians, the first group of them is individual in its emphasis. Galatians 2:16 states that "a man is not justified by the works of the law." The offender against the law of God cannot compensate for his offense by good deeds performed subsequent to his offense. There are two reasons for this conclusion. First of all, if a man argues on the basis of the law, he must abide by legal procedure in order to be consistent. Law knows no exceptions; it makes obedience obligatory at all times. Complete obedience to the law is expected of everyone; and therefore there cannot be a superfluity of obedience on one occasion that can counterbalance a disobedience on a previous occasion. If perfect obedience is expected at all times, any offense is consequently irreparable.

Second, disobedience is not a single act unattended by any result to the perpetrator other than the penalty inflicted from without. Sin affects the man himself, and renders him at once incapable of complete obedience because the habit of sin has begun. One sin always leads to another; sin produces a chain reaction. Imperfect man, with the record and habit of sin, is thus unable to retrace his steps to complete righteousness. He is in the position of a person whose income exactly equals his expenses, and who has been injured in an accident in which he owes heavy damages. Because his expenses are normally equal to his income he can never repay the damages; and if he does not have proper medical care, however costly it may be, he will never be able to earn even his daily living. Similarly a salvation dependent upon works is a bankrupt salvation.

The solution to this dismal situation appears in the next clauses of the same verse (2:16). "We believed on Christ Jesus, that we might be justified by faith in Christ, and not by the works of the law." Justification by faith in Christ means that the believer trusts Christ to do for him what he cannot do for himself. Christ's righteousness succeeded where human righteousness failed. When He was subjected to temptation like ours, He did not yield. He always did the things that pleased God, whereas we disobeyed God. He died, not because He deserved death for His own sins, but rather to take part in our lot and to deliver us. As Peter said, "Christ also suffered for sins once, the righteous for the unrighteous, that he might bring us to God" (I Peter 3:18).

Again, if men are found sinners while seeking to be justified, does that make Christ a promoter of sin (2:17)? Is He simply providing an easy method of escape for those who deserve punishment? Not at all! He is exemplifying grace, by meeting sinners where they are and by saving them. If He waited until they had struggled out of sin and had perfected themselves, they would never be saved, for they could not attain such a victory by their own strength. Justification is not simply an escape from sin; it is deliverance from sin. It means not only remission of punishment, but means also a new stand-

ing of the believer with God and a clean break with the evil
that had previously made the future hopeless.

This passage in 2:16, 17 is closely connected with 2:20,
which speaks of the new inner life of the believer — "Christ
liveth in me." Thus justification leads naturally into sancti-
fication, and into the new life which tends away from evil unto God. The passage as a whole sets the doctrinal keynote
for the book; and the theological argument of 3:1 to 4:31
follows the general pattern of its thought.

The second group of passages, 3:8, 11, and 24, treat of the
historical background of justification in the Old Testament.
Justification, according to Paul, is not a freakish novelty which
he had invented. It was predicted as far back as the days of
Abraham, when God promised His blessings to the Gentiles by
telling Abraham that in his seed all the nations of the earth
should be blessed (Gen. 12:1-3). These blessings could not
be bestowed by the law because all who did not keep the law
were under a curse. If Jews or Gentiles who were disobedient
to the law were under a curse, they were not eligible for a blessing. Consequently, the blessing could be bestowed on them
only by some method other than the operation of law. The
law compelled men to look for another means of becoming
righteous in God's sight, and made faith the necessary alternative to legalism.

Justification, therefore, is contrasted with legalism, which
operates from cause to effect. According to the law, the sinner was placed under a penalty from which the law was powerless to deliver him. In the reign of moral cause and effect
there could be no exceptions. Grace, however, introduced a
new power to offset the old cause, and to produce a new effect;
for grace can forgive sin, and so can pave the way for a
growth in righteousness.

Under the dispensation of grace, the true value of the law
became apparent. Instead of being a system to be observed as
an end in itself, its function was understood as preparatory

and disciplinary. Paul said, "The law is become our tutor *to bring us* unto Christ, that we might be justified by faith" (Gal. 3 :24). The law served the purpose of leading men up to justification by faith, but was not intended to take its place. In this way, justification by faith is explained as the goal of a trend in God's plan as well as a cardinal principle in His present mode of action.

The most direct use of the verb *dikaioo* occurs in 5 :4 where it introduces the final appeal of the book. "Ye are severed from Christ, ye who would be justified by the law; ye are fallen away from grace." Paul insisted that justification by faith and justification by law are diametrically opposed to each other, and that to return to legalism is to abandon Christ. These words are the introduction to the practical section of Galatians, in which the personal outcome of justification is treated at length. Justification by faith is shown to be the introduction to the true life of freedom, which is also the life of fruitfulness.

The study of this word in its context shows how deeply rooted it is in the thought of the epistle as a whole. The similar study of any other important doctrinal term, such as faith, would also give a key to the thought of the epistle from a different approach.

The Doctrinal Section of the Book

The doctrinal section of Galatians commences with the opening of the third chapter and extends through the fourth chapter. This is the heart of the book. The central question of Galatians is doctrinal: Are men made right with God by the careful discharge of a certain series of duties or by observing certain ceremonial formulas, or are they made right with God solely by trusting in what Christ is and in what He has done?

The answer to this question is presented by seven main arguments:

1. From personal experience 3:1-5
2. From Old Testament teaching 3:6-14
3. From priority of promise 3:15-22
4. From superiority of maturity in Christ....3:23-4:7
5. From danger of reaction 4:8-11
6. From contrast of motives 4:12-20
7. From contrast of bondage and liberty 4:21-31

The Argument from Personal Experience 3:1-5

Personal experience is not the final criterion of doctrinal truth, because no man's experience is so general, so unprejudiced, and so free from imperfections that it can become a universal pattern for all other men. Revelation alone can determine the final norm of doctrine. Nevertheless, personal experience is a potent factor in judging any question, because whatever has actually entered into human life has ceased to be a theory. Lest the issue of law and grace should seem to be purely abstract and unrelated to common life, Paul has connected it with actual human experience by certain pointed questions:

1. Did the Galatians receive the Holy Spirit by the works of the law or by the hearing of faith?
2. Can the initial experience of life in the Spirit be brought to maturity by the flesh? (*i.e.,* Can the motive of the law be a fitting climax for the spontaneous work of the Holy Spirit?)
3. Is the work of the Spirit in the lives of believers to be abandoned as futile, and should there be a return to the law?
4. Does the miraculous work of the Spirit in the church depend upon the works of the law or upon the hearing of faith?

With these four questions, paraphrased from the text of Galatians, the doctrinal argument is opened. The questions are directed to the personal experience of the Galatian Christians, and assume certain facts. They take for granted (1) that the personal incoming of the Holy Spirit into the life of a believer is the token that gives him assurance of his acceptance with God; (2) that the continuity of this life is dependent on the further work of the Spirit, and that it cannot be developed by self-effort (the flesh); (3) that the spiritual struggles through which the Galatians have passed would warrant maintaining the progress of faith to the end; and (4) that the Holy Spirit was still performing miraculous deeds among them such as had never been produced by the law. These four criteria are regarded as normal to Christian life, and are points of appeal in Paul's remonstrance to the church. Their implications are discussed at greater length in the practical section of the epistle.

The Argument from Old Testament Teaching 3:6-14

The Scriptural standard for evaluating the doctrine of salvation by faith is the record of the Old Testament concerning Abraham. There are several reasons why the example of Abraham is applicable to this question. Abraham was "the friend of God" (Jas. 2:23), and is one of the few characters in the Old Testament whose spiritual experience is given in sufficient detail to constitute a pattern for the New Testament believer. Those that are of faith are sons of Abraham in the sense that their spiritual careers are modeled upon his. Again, the first advance of God to any group after the devastating judgment of the Flood was centered in Abraham. To him was the promise given that established the Messianic expectation of the new world, and from him originated the people who became the vehicle of God's purpose and promise. Third, the promise given to Abraham antedated the giving of the law, and so took priority over it. Fourth, the Judaizing faction in Galatia probably appealed to Abraham as one of the links in their historical argument for the necessity of circumcision, since God had introduced it to Abraham in conjunction with the confirmation of the covenant. If Paul could use the Judaizers' illustration against them, he would have scored a triumph in debate.

In the process of this doctrinal argument the experience of Abraham is cited as part of Scripture, not simply as the exemplary experience of a good man. In verses 8, 10, 11, and 22 Paul stressed the authority of the written record and accepted it as final. He sought the solution of the problem not in a vote expressive of the church's opinion, but in the interpretation of the divine revelation.

The Scriptural argument, then, is regarded as an advance on the personal and practical argument suggested in the introductory questions of chapter three. It is as follows:

1. The basic principle of spiritual experience as exemplified in Abraham was: "Abraham believed God, and it was reckoned unto him for righteousness" (Gal. 3:6).

2. Those who take their stand on the same principle are "sons of Abraham," that is, they are his successors in the life of faith, and are eligible for the same spiritual blessings that God gave to him.

3. God promised to Abraham that in him all the Gentiles should be blessed.

4. Therefore those Gentiles that take their stand on faith in the promises of God are candidates for blessing with Abraham.

5. Conversely, those under the law are cursed, because:

   a. The law pronounces a curse on all those that do not observe its every precept.

   b. The implication (explicit in Romans 3:23) is that none have kept the law perfectly: therefore

   c. All are under its curse.

6. Furthermore, salvation by the law and salvation by faith are mutually exclusive; for

    a. If "the righteous shall live by faith," and

    b. If the law is not of faith, but of works, then

    c. Those under the law do not receive the blessings of faith.

7. Consequently, the only way to enjoy the fulness of the life of God is to abandon the law as a system of salvation, and to trust in Christ, who has taken upon Himself the curse of the law, that the promise of the Spirit might come upon all through faith.

The Argument from Priority of Promise 3:15-22

The foregoing argument, which is a summary of Galatians 3:6-14, leaves one or two questions still to be settled.

First, what is the relation of the covenant with Abraham to the law which is admittedly a revelation of God? Second, what was the function of the law? Was it useless?

Paul pointed out that even human covenants between man and man are regarded as inviolate and unalterable, and that when they are once concluded they are not susceptible of change. How much more sacred, then, would be a covenant between God and man! If God concluded a covenant of promise with Abraham, the law which was given four hundred and thirty years afterward could not alter it, and would not supplant it. If inheritance came by law it would not be by promise; and God had already guaranteed the inheritance on the basis of promise. If the law was antedated by the promise, the latter should be regarded as having superior validity.

If, on the other hand, the law was the definite gift of God, as Scripture says it is, how could it be set aside lightly? The answer is that the law was given for a dual purpose: to restrain the wickedness of men until the promise could be fulfilled, and to reveal to men their need of a work of grace that would transcend the law itself (Gal. 3:19, 22).

If no restraint had been placed upon men, degeneration would have been swift and disastrous. Even with the knowledge of the law Israel lapsed repeatedly into sin. Had there been no expressed standard, with its prohibitions and punishments, there could have been no proper background for the promised Seed when He did come.

Furthermore, the function of the law in the individual was the creation of the awareness of sin. Paul himself said, "I had not known sin, except through the law" (Romans 7:7). The high demands of the law, and the consequent realization of failure that haunted every conscientious Jew who tried in vain to keep it, demonstrated clearly the necessity of a promise which could be given to those who believed. Of such a class, undoubtedly, were those whom Luke mentioned as "righteous and devout, looking for the consolation of Israel" (Luke 2:25). To them the law was an ultimate blessing, not because it satisfied their needs directly but because it made them reach out in faith to the Messiah when He finally came.

The function of the law, was preparatory and temporary. God never intended it to be His final method of saving men; indeed, the very sacrifices stipulated by the law were an admission of its imperfection, for they would not have been necessary had man been able to keep the law perfectly by his own unaided strength. On the other hand, the law was a revelation of God's inflexible holiness that requires man to meet His standards if man would know Him and enjoy eternal life. It was intended to act as a regulative and restraining influence upon human life between the promise of God and the fulfillment of that promise.

The Argument from Superiority of Maturity in Christ 3:23-4:7

Under the regime of law all spiritual life was regulated by precept and rule. To be sure, the law took cognizance of love as the deepest and truest aspect of spiritual life. Jesus, when asked by a harassed and bewildered legalist what the greatest commandment of all was, quoted Deuteronomy 6:5: "Thou shalt love Jehovah thy God with all thy heart, and with all thy soul, and with all thy might."

The majority of devout Jews in His day, however, thought of the law as a taskmaster, whose orders must be obeyed for fear of the penalty of infringement. Paul compared the situation to that in a household where the children are under the care of a *paidagogos,* usually an old slave, who was charged with the responsibility of preparing them for school and of hurrying them safely off to the schoolmaster lest they loiter on the way or be endangered by the traffic of the streets. When they reached the schoolmaster the responsibilities of the *paidagogos* ended. So with the law, its authority ended when it had brought men to Christ.

The figure of the household is carried still farther by Paul to show that the law is for the immature in the knowledge of God, while faith is a sign of maturity. The child who is under the guardians and stewards appointed by the father is, as far as his actual position is concerned, a slave. He cannot assert his own will; he cannot hold his own property; he cannot marry when he will; everything is prescribed for him. On the day when he formally comes of age, the father recognizes him as an equal, and delegates to him the right to administer his own life. "So we also, when we were children, were held in bondage under the rudiments of the world: but when the fulness of the time came, God sent forth his Son . . . that he might redeem them that were under the law, that we might receive the adoption [2] of sons" (Gal. 4:3-5). This sonship is achieved through faith, which brings sons out from under the law into the liberty of full-grown members of God's family. Four consequences of this relationship at once become apparent:

1. The sons are emancipated from the law, and no longer need to recognize its direct authority on their lives (Gal. 3:25).

2. The sons pass beyond the dividing line which the law drew between Jew and Gentile. All class distinctions disappear in the new fraternal life in Christ (Gal. 3:28).

---

2. The term "adoption" (*huiothesia*) may have two separate interpretations. The usual meaning is that a child is accepted into a family to which he is unrelated by blood, and that he is given all of the rights and privileges of a son, including heirship. This is the common meaning in the papyri. Moulton & Milligan, *op. cit., in loco*, cite from one of the papyri, P Oxy IX. 1206[8], which says: "We agree, Heracles and his wife Isarion on the one part, that we have given away to you, Horion, for adoption our son Patermouthis, aged about two years, and I Horion on the other part, that I have him as my own son so that the rights proceeding from succession to my inheritance shall be maintained for him."

The other interpretation is that *huiothesia* applies to the public recognition of a son by his father when he promotes him to full heirship. L. S. Chafer, in his *Systematic Theology* (Dallas, Texas: Dallas Seminary Press, 1948) III, 242, regards the term as given a new meaning quite different from that of the current use. "According to human custom, adoption is a means whereby an outsider can become a member of a family . . . On the other hand, divine adoption . . . is primarily a divine act by which one already a child by actual birth through the Spirit of God is placed forward as an adult son in his relation to God."

The former interpretation agrees better with the use of *huiothesia* in the vernacular of Paul's day, and has the support of most commentators. The latter interpretation seems to fit better the language of the context, and accords reasonably well with the other usages which occur in the New Testament. All these usages occur in the Pauline epistles: Gal. 4:5, Rom. 8:15, 23; 9:4; Eph. 1:5. The crux of interpretation is whether Paul were adhering strictly to the ordinary use of the word, or whether he were using it as a technical theological term to denote a new doctrinal concept. In any case, his emphasis was on the dignity and permanence of the sonship which the believer has in Christ.

For the former interpretation, see C. J. Ellicott, *A Critical and Grammatical Commentary on St. Paul's Epistle to the Galatians* (Boston: Draper & Halliday, 1866), I, 94. For a somewhat different interpretation, cf. Ramsay's *Historical Commentary on Galatians*, pp. 391-393.

3. As sons enjoying full liberties, they become heirs who are entitled to all that the Father's resources can give them (Gal. 3:29).

4. The consciousness of sonship is created in each individual's heart by the Holy Spirit (Gal. 4:6). The appearance of the Seed, Christ, brought the fulfillment of the promise and the consequent termination of law. For Gentile and Jew alike He is the redemptive answer to man's ethical plight, for He was born under the law that He might redeem those under the law, that they might receive the adoption of sons. This position of maturity in Christ is far better than that of immature childhood which the law assumed and perpetuated. Why should the Galatians desire to revert to the status of childhood when they now possessed adult freedom in Christ?

The Argument from Danger of Reaction 4:8-11

In the first seven verses of Galatians 4 Paul was dealing with Jews when he said, "So we also, when we were children, were held in bondage under the rudiments of the world" (4:3). The word "we" shows that he classed himself among those whom he was addressing, and the resumption of the "we" in verse five, "that he might redeem them that were under the law, that we might receive the adoption of sons," indicates that he had been "under the law." Only Jews could be said to be under the law; the Gentiles were not.[3] The word "rudiments" in this passage (4:3), therefore, refers to the law.

In the next paragraph (Gal. 4:8-11), however, the word "rudiments" [4] is applied to the Gentile, for Paul said "ye," not

---

3. Cf. Romans 2:14.
4. Greek: *stoicheia.* The word originally meant "row," or "rank," and was applied to the list of the letters of the alphabet. Hence it came to mean rudimentary knowledge, or the first principles of any subject. (Cf. Heb. 5:12) Moulton & Milligan, *op. cit., in loco.* cite F. H. Colson and W. H. P. Hatch as suggesting that the *stoicheia* of Gal. 4:3 and Col. 2:8 may refer to the "seven planets" or to "personal cosmic powers," heathen deities whom the pagans held in reverence.

"we." The Gentiles were formerly ignorant of God and were "in bondage to them that by nature are no gods." Such language could scarcely be used of Israelites who had known the true God and who had not been accustomed to serving pagan deities. Both Jewish and Gentile members of the Galatian churches had reverted to the past when they went back to the law for their spiritual perfection.

The "rudiments" to which they returned seem to have been ceremonial observances. Such rites could never be in themselves the reality of spiritual things. They could only foreshadow or typify certain realities. The "days, and months, and seasons, and years" were commemorative of certain historical experiences or emblematic of the approach to God; but the celebration of these occasions did not actually bring the celebrants closer to God. Paul charged the Gentile Christians with going back to the old principle of ritual observance and works as a means of spiritual perfection — a concept diametrically opposed to the principle of salvation by grace. If the Gentile Christians adopted the Jewish legalism, they would be taking Jewish ceremonialism as a replacement for pagan ceremonialism. The former might be superior to the latter in its central theism and in its purer morality, but both would be equally deficient in power to reconcile a sinner to God or to perfect him in the knowledge of God.

Such a reaction from the higher way of faith back to the old way of ritual could have only a damaging effect on the lives of the Galatians. There is no spiritual darkness more dense than the darkness brought on by light rejected. The return to bondage would be fatal to spiritual progress, and would produce a result quite opposite to that which the Galatians sought in turning to legalism for perfection.

The Argument from Contrast of Motives 4:12-20

The paragraph contained in verses 12 through 20 inclusive is a study in contrasting motives. If the Galatians were willing to evaluate the alternate messages of liberty and legalism in terms of the motives of their respective religious proponents, Paul had another ground of appeal. He asked them to look at the question from his viewpoint, since he had looked at it from theirs. He pointed out to them that he preached at the outset in weakness and in illness, not for personal gain. They had accepted his message as sincere, and they had accorded to him a sympathetic hearing. Not only had they refrained from recoiling in disgust from his malady which would naturally cause them to shun him, but they had received him as an angel of God. They had hung on his words and had accepted his message. Since that time his motives had not changed. Why should they now question his sincerity and reject the message which they had so eagerly welcomed under less favorable circumstances?

On the other hand, the motives of his opponents would not bear scrutiny. Their legalism was not prompted by a passion for truth, but it was the result of religious snobbery. Strict obedience to the letter of the law was regarded as the mark of a superior class. All others who did not hold legalism as the key to perfection were excluded from the small circle of the righteous, and were, by the very assumption of exclusivism, challenged to seek perfection on the terms of the legalists. Paul thus asserted that love was his motive for preaching liberty in Christ, while the Judaizers' motive for insisting on circumcision was a haughty exclusivism.

The Argument from the Contrast of Bondage
and Liberty 4:21-31

The literary interpretation of this paragraph will be reserved for another chapter, for it belongs in the realm of allegory. Its obvious intent is this: If Hagar, the slave woman, represents Mt. Sinai, the place where the law was given, and if Sarah, the freewoman, represents faith, then the slave woman is inferior to the freewoman, and is to be rejected while the freewoman retains her place of honor; so legalism is to be repudiated and the way of faith is to be cherished. Furthermore, as the son of the handmaid persecuted the son of the freewoman, so the legalist persecutes the man of faith. Paul boldly asserted that believers are the sons of the freewoman, and that they are the children of the Spirit, whereas the others are still children of the flesh. So the believer in Christ is to repudiate the bondage of the law, and is to live in the freedom of the Spirit.

With this final argument Paul concluded his case for faith versus works. The challenge to the personal experience of the Galatians aroused them to reconsider their past dealings with God and consequently to revaluate the present situation. With the background of the authority of the Scriptures, and with the historical precedents contained in them, these Christians would see that the doctrine of justification by faith was antecedent to the law and that it was firmly established as a truth. In addition, it promised greater blessings to the individual believer who could take his stand as an heir of God and who could claim blessings from God that could never have come through the law. To embrace legalism would not be a step forward, but would be a reversion to paganism, with its futile ceremonies and useless negations. The legalists sought only to enhance their own following. The alternative before the Galatians was bondage or freedom; and Paul spared no effort to make the issue clear, and to persuade them to make the right choice.

THE ART OF EXPRESSING TRUTH

The Rhetorical Method

CHAPTER VI

THE ART OF EXPRESSING TRUTH

THE RHETORICAL METHOD

S INCE the Bible is the Word of God to man, its truth is expressed in human language in order to make it understandable; for an incomprehensible revelation would be of no value at all. Truth, in order to be effective, must be stated in the everyday terms that people use. Sometimes, however, there are no words for conveying exactly the meaning of an abstract concept. It may be so novel that no vocabulary for it has been developed, or it may be so complex that no one expression can contain all of it. When such a situation occurs, figures of speech generally are employed to state the unknown in terms of the known.

Figures of Speech

All great literature contains figurative speech; and the Bible is no exception. Sometimes the vividness of an idea is heightened by the use of a comparison, or the true character of some person or concept is brought out by the figure employed. Abstract spiritual ideas have been expressed best by metaphors which, as time has gone on, have become fixed theological terms. Paul used many figures of speech in Galatians, and not a few of the important teachings of the book are conveyed through symbolic language. Because a correct interpretation of the book is dependent upon an understanding of those figures, a few of them will be treated representatively so that the reader may find others and interpret them for himself.

Classification

The classification of these figures of speech is as follows:[1]

1. Figures of color, determined by the use of the imagination in connecting the literal fact with its figurative expression.
2. Figures of form, which are created by the use and arrangement of words in their relation to each other.
3. Figures of analogy of words, which depend for their effectiveness upon external likeness of the words involved, irrespective of their meaning.

Figures of color are most frequently used and easiest to define. Among them are

1. *Simile* — an expressed comparison between two objects which are materially unrelated to each other.
2. *Metaphor* — a comparison between two objects suggested by the substitution of the name of the one for the name of the other.
3. *Allegory* — an extended simile or metaphor by which the details of a story are made to convey a meaning different from the literal meaning of the events recorded.
4. *Metonymy* — the use of a word for another that it suggests, as the effect for the cause or the cause for the effect.
5. *Synecdoche* — the use of a part to represent the whole or the use of the whole to represent the part.
6. *Hyperbole* — exaggeration for the sake of emphasis.

Figures of form can be multiplied almost indefinitely in any piece of literature if any departure from strict literality of expression is called a figure. The Greek rhetoricians had a name

---

1. The classification is with some modifications taken from F. W. Farrar, "The Rhetoric of St. Paul," *Expositor*, Series I, X (1879), 1-27.

for almost every kind of turn of thought, but only five of these deserve special mention in Galatians.

1. *Irony* — a statement which is made contrary to existing fact in order to emphasize its actuality.

2. *Litotes* — the affirmation of a fact by denying its opposite.

3. *Meiosis* — an understatement of truth for the sake of emphasis, the opposite of hyperbole.

4. *Euphemism* — the substitution of a mild expression for a term that might be violent or coarse, although the significance of the literal fact is attached to it.

5. *Rhetorical Question* — the use of a question which calls for no direct answer, in order to attract the attention of the hearer.

Figures of color and figures of form are common to almost all literature, and can be reproduced even in translation. They appear in Galatians, and may be detected quite readily in the English text. The figures of the third classification cannot be carried over in translation, since resemblance of any two or more words in Greek does not mean necessarily that the English terms by which they are translated will be alike. Figures of analogy of words, therefore, are deliberately omitted from this treatment because they have no bearing on practical interpretation.

Distribution

The accompanying chart is not an exhaustive catalog of all the figures of speech that appear in Galatians, but it does include the majority of the more important usages. The passages are not quoted in full, but a catch phrase is given for the purpose of identification. The main divisions of the outline are reproduced in order that the distribution of the figures in the several sections of Galatians may be clearly apparent. The

FIGURES OF SPEECH IN GALATIANS

FIGURES	THE DIVISIONS OF GALATIANS				
Figures of Color	Introduction 1:1-9	I. The Biographical Argument 1:10-2:21	II. The Theological Argument 3:1-4:31	III. The Practical Argument 5:1-6:10	Conclusion 6:11-18
1. Simile			3:6 Even as Abraham 4:3 So also we . . . 4:14 received me as an angel		
2. Metaphor		1:10 slave* of Christ 2:9 pillars	3:1 bewitched openly set forth 3:13 redeemed 3:24 tutor 3:27 put on Christ 4:8 bondage 4:19 in travail	5:1 yoke of bondage 5:3 debtor 5:7 running well 5:9 leaven 5:11 stumblingblock 5:13 servants 5:15 bite and devour 5:16 walk 5:22 fruit of Spirit 6:5 burden 6:7 sowing and reaping 6:10 household of faith	6:17 branded
3. Allegory			4:21-31 Two sons		
4. Metonymy		1:22 churches of Judea 2:9 circumcision	3:13 tree 3:19 seed		6:12 cross of Christ
5. Synecdoche		1:16 flesh and blood 2:16 flesh	3:1 before whose eyes	5:13 flesh	
6. Hyperbole	1:8 we, or an angel from heaven		4:15 ye would have plucked out your eyes	5:12 go beyond circumcision	
Figures of Form					
1. Irony			4:18 but it is good . . . with you		
2. Litotes			4:17 in no good way	5:10 none otherwise minded	
3. Meiosis				5:23 against such there is no law	
4. Euphemism				5:12 go beyond circumcision (not in Greek)	
5. Rhetorical Question	1:10 am I now seeking . . . or am I striving		3:1 Who did bewitch 3:2 Received ye the Spirit? 3:3 Are ye so foolish Are ye now perfected 3:4 Did ye suffer 3:5 Doeth he it by the works of the law 3:21 Is the law then 4:15 Where then is that gratulation 4:16 Am I become your enemy	5:7 who hindered you	
		*Greek: doulos			

largest number of the figures occur in the theological and practical arguments in which Paul utilized every available method to convince the Galatians of their errors. To Paul they were the weapons of thought by which he attacked the opposition, not ornaments to be used for the rhetorical decoration of his writing.

The figures of speech offer several avenues of approach to the study of Galatians. First of all, they afford some insight into the mind and temperament of the author. The largest number of metaphors were taken from social phenomena. Paul did not utilize the illustrations from nature that appeared in the discourses of Jesus, nor did he refer to agricultural life as James did. Several of his metaphors were drawn from the institution of slavery (1:10; 5:1, 13); some were taken from family life (6:10); one, at least, was borrowed from the superstitions of the day (3:1); another, from clothing (3:27); another, from shipping (6:5); another, from athletics (5:7). In these figures Paul's diversified interests and contacts are preserved; for the illustrations that a man uses most naturally are those that grow out of his occupation or out of his personal observation. They show that Paul's background was chiefly urban.

These devices, however, are not employed artificially solely for the sake of effect. They fit naturally into the argument of the epistle, and illumine its more complicated turns of thought. If the figures of speech were all removed from Galatians, the book would be much more prosy and less forceful at the very points where vividness is most needed for driving home the truth which it was written to maintain.

Two groups of these figures appear in the epistle, as the chart reveals. One is a series of rhetorical questions at the beginning of the third chapter. After demonstrating that his personal career was in entire accord with the doctrine of justification by faith, Paul sought to arouse his readers to think of their own needs. He wished to present the issue as sharp-

ly as possible. The rapid succession of six rhetorical questions, like as many trumpet blasts, defines the question of debate and states the criteria by which the question should be
judged. If the epistle were read to the churches in their meet-
ings rather than read by the individual members in succession,
the questions would be all the more arresting in their effect.

The second group of figures is a long series of metaphors
in the fifth chapter between verses 1 and 22. Around them is
organized the practical argument of Galatians. They illustrate the principal points of the relation of this argument to
Christian conduct: emancipation from the law as the main-
spring of new and productive spiritual life; the relation of
emancipated persons to each other; and the contrasting effects
of the walk in the flesh and the walk in the Spirit.

The value of the individual figures of speech will be treated
in the following paragraphs by a presentation of one of each
kind listed in the chart. No complete exposition of them all
is proposed, but specimens are given in order that the method
of rhetorical interpretation may be demonstrated.

Explanation: Figures of Color
1. *Simile*

"Ye received me as an angel of God . . ."   (4:14)

This simile occurs in Paul's remonstrance with the Galatians concerning the change in their attitude toward him. On
his first visit to them, occasioned by sickness which made him
appear at his worst, they had received him as if he were an
angel of God. Perhaps he was thinking of the account in
Genesis 18 concerning Abraham's hospitable reception of the
visitors who turned out to be angels, or perhaps he was using
the simile without any allusion to the Old Testament story.
In any case, it implies that the Galatians had honored him as
a distinguished guest, and that they had given great deference
to his spiritual authority. His feeling for them had not
changed; but their reversal of attitude is reflected in his ques-

tion: "So then am I become your enemy, by telling you the truth?" (4:16)

2. Metaphor

> *For freedom did Christ set us free: stand fast therefore, and be not entangled again in a yoke of bondage.*
> (5:1)

One of the most vivid metaphors of Paul is the term "yoke of bondage" which he applied to legalism. The word appears six times in the New Testament: twice in Matthew 11:29, 30, where it is figurative of discipline and of the instrument by which effort is made useful; three times in the Lukan and Pauline writings (Acts 15:10, Gal. 5:1, I Tim. 6:1), where it bears the connotation of slavery; and once in Revelation 6:5, where it means "balance" or "scales." The passage in Acts 15:10 is parallel to Galatians 5:1, for there Peter applied the term to the law as "a yoke . . . which neither our fathers nor we were able to bear." Both in Acts and in Galatians the figure is applied to the law, and the "yoke" is represented as an intolerable burden which enslaves and crushes the one upon whom it is placed. Galatians 5:1 is the essence of the whole argument of the epistle, concentrated into a final application which this vigorous metaphor makes doubly convincing.

3. Allegory

> *Tell me, ye that desire to be under the law, do ye not hear the law? For it is written, that Abraham had two sons, one by the handmaid, and one by the freewoman. Howbeit the son by the handmaid is born after the flesh; but the son by the freewoman is born through promise. Which things contain an allegory: for these women are two covenants; one from mount Sinai, bearing children unto bondage, which is Hagar. Now this Hagar is mount Sinai in Arabia, and answereth to the Jerusalem that now is: for she is in bondage with her children. But the Jerusalem that is above is free, which is our mother. For it is written,*

Rejoice, thou barren that bearest not;
Break forth and cry, thou that travailest not:
For more are the children of the desolate than of her that
hath the husband.

Now we, brethren, as Isaac was, are children of promise.
But as then he that was born after the flesh persecuted him
that was born *after the Spirit, so also it is now, Howbeit*
what saith the scripture? Cast out the handmaid and her
son: for the son of the handmaid shall not inherit with the
son of the freewoman. Wherefore, brethren, we are not
children of a handmaid, but of the freewoman.

(4:21-31)

One of the most controversial points of exegesis in Galatians is the allegory of 4:21-31. Was it original with Paul,
or did he borrow it from the rabbinical background in which
he had been trained? Did he mean by the clause, "which
things contain an allegory" (4:24),[2] that the text of Genesis
was intended as an allegory and not as sober history, or that
he had simply used it allegorically to illustrate spiritual truth?
Did he intend to convey the idea that all of the Old Testament
may be or should be interpreted allegorically and that the true
meaning could be achieved only by so understanding it; or did
he use the allegory simply because it was a common device of
his day which his readers would accept more readily than a
more abstract, though perhaps a more logical, argument?

In answering these questions one should remember that the
rabbinic method of interpretation often went to extremes in
drawing conclusions from real or fancied implications in historical truth, and that Jewish teaching of the more mystical
school frequently resorted to allegorical interpretation. Paul
seldom used allegory, and always without fanciful or fantastic
import. He argued often from historical precedent, as he did in
Galatians 3 from the story of Abraham; and sometimes his
philological interpretation seemed at first sight to be a bit

2. Greek: *allegoroumena.* Used only here in the New Testament. For
a full discussion of this term, see Burton, *op. cit.,* 254-257.

strained, as in his distinction between *seeds* and *seed*: "He saith not, And to seeds, as of many; but as of one, And to thy seed, which is Christ" (3:16). He was quite sparing of the allegorical technique which was used much by Philo of Alexandria and later by Origen, and he was free from the abuse of that method which is apparent in their writings.

The allegory in this passage is introduced by two explanatory statements:

> *Tell me, ye that desire to be under the law, do ye not hear the law?*
>
> (4:21)
>
> *Which things contain an allegory: for these* women *are two covenants; one from mount Sinai, bearing children unto bondage, which is Hagar.*
>
> (4:24)

The first statement indicates that the allegory is not to be superimposed upon the historical narrative as a strait jacket, in an attempt to force it to say what it does not. Paul felt that by the allegorical application of the narrative of Genesis he was bringing out clearly the spiritual truth which was inherent in it anyway. Nowhere did he intimate that the literal history was unimportant or untrue. On the contrary, he assumed its actuality when he said: "For it is written, that Abraham had two sons, one by the handmaid, and one by the freewoman" (4:22).

The second statement should then be understood to mean that the principle in the historic fact could best be applied to the Galatian crisis by making it allegorical of the two covenents of law and grace. Hagar, who was the bondmaid, was under the law of slavery. Her son was born in accordance with law, but of the desire expressed in natural generation [3] rather than by the gift and will of God. Sarah, who was the freewoman, bore her son as the result of God's miraculous

---

3. See Gal. 4:23. Greek: *kata sarka,* "after the flesh." Cf. Rom. 1:3, 9:5, where *kata sarka* refers to physical birth.

grace revealed in creative life. As the son of the slave woman could not succeed to the inheritance of the father after
the son of the freewoman was born, so those who seek to maintain spiritual life by the law have no claim on the riches which
fall to those who are heirs of promise. Furthermore, as the
son of the handmaid mocked the son of the freewoman,[4] so
hostility between the legalist and the believer in grace may be
expected.

The value of this allegory to the practical argument is two-
fold: (1) it enforces the principle of grace by citation from
the law, which was the legalist's chief authority; and (2) it
employed the method of interpretation which the Jewish and
rabbinical school used very frequently. If the Judaizers relied
upon any allegorizing of the law for their purposes, Paul answered them by their own method, much as the Lord answered
the Sadducees in replying to them from the books of Moses,
the only Scripture which they held to be inspired (Matt. 22:
23-37).

4. Metonymy

> But far be it from me to glory, save in the cross of our
> Lord Jesus Christ, through which the world hath been
> crucified unto me, and I unto the world.
>
> (6:14)

Perhaps the best illustration of metonymy in Galatians is
the word *cross* (5:11; 6:12, 14). Paul's use of the term was
seldom literal, although, of course, he adhered to historic reality. Only in two or three passages (Phil. 2:8; Col. 1:20;
2:14) did he seem to refer directly to the material cross of
wood; and even in these instances its spiritual significance was
stressed.

In Galatians *cross* stands for all that the death of Christ
achieved and represented. Paul spoke of it as "the stumbling-
block of the cross" (5:11), of being "persecuted for the cross

---

4. Cf. Gal. 4:29 and Gen. 21:9.

of Christ" (6:12), and of glorying "in the cross of our Lord Jesus Christ" (6:14). Each of these passages represents the principle or the body of truth which contains the meaning of the cross.

"The stumbling-block of the cross" means literally "the scandal of the cross." The Greek word *skandalon*, translated "stumbling-block," meant originally "the trigger of a trap." It came to mean anything by which embarrassment or shame might be brought upon a person. Paul's language implied that the death of Christ posed a question in the minds of both Gentile and Jew that often kept them from Christ. If He were put to death by the method which was reserved usually for slaves and criminals, how could He be regarded as personally righteous, under the blessing of God? If He were incapable of rescuing Himself from the hands of His enemies, how could He save men by His merits and by His relation to God? Because of the cross His claims were unbelievable to the Jew, who regarded Him as under a curse because He was hanged on a tree;[5] and His claims were unacceptable to the Gentile, who regarded the idea of a crucified savior as utterly irrational.[6]

Galatians 6:12 uses the term "cross" as the symbol for the whole system of Christian belief and for the idea of salvation by grace in particular. If the cross be accepted as God's method of salvation, then all human righteousness is valueless and all human works are futile as a means of insuring salvation. The cross had condemned them all. Naturally such an attitude to human works is a blow to human pride; and wounded pride retaliates with persecution. Those who do not wish to endure the persecution seek some way of avoiding the cross and its application to their lives. This explains the Judaizers' effort not only to escape it themselves, but to compel all others to follow along with them.

---

5. Gal. 3:13.
6. I Cor. 1:22-24.

The third and last use of this metonym in Galatians is in 6:14: "But far be it from me to glory, save in the cross of our Lord Jesus Christ, through which the world hath been crucified unto me, and I unto the world." To Paul the cross was not a symbol of shame but of liberation. Because it dealt so thoroughly with sin and with the flesh, its efforts far transcended those of legalism which was symbolized by circumcision. The cross dealt with the inner life; circumcision, as advocated by the Judaizers, affected only the outward flesh. Paul boasted not in his own righteousness, but in the work of Christ for him and in him, which work was summed up in the "cross."

5. *Synecdoche*

> *Straightway I conferred not with flesh and blood.*
> (1:16)

Synecdoche is a common figure in everyday speech, such as "hands" instead of workers, "sails" for ships, and "brains" instead of scholars. It is used only a few times in Galatians. The most striking of these instances occurs in 1:16, where Paul says that after his conversion he "conferred not with flesh and blood." By the phrase "flesh and blood" he meant human beings in terms of their tangible bodily substance. Wherever this particular phrase is used in the New Testament, it generally connotes the idea of mere humanity as opposed to deity or to supernatural beings.[7] Paul's whole point in Galatians 1:16 is that he did not owe his message to any secondary human source, but that he had received it directly from the revelation which God had sent. This use of synecdoche serves to make the contrast all the more emphatic.

6. *Hyperbole*

> *But though we, or an angel from heaven, should preach unto you any gospel other than that which we preached unto you, let him be anathema.* (1:8)

---

7. Cf. Matt. 16:17; John 1:13; I Cor. 15:50; Eph. 6:12; Heb. 2:14.

The use of hyperbole, which is exaggeration for the sake of effect, might naturally be expected in an epistle so important and so vehement as Galatians. Controversialists do not often use moderate language; and Paul was certainly a controversialist. Only three instances of direct hyperbole can be found in Galatians,[8] of which the first is the best example.

In all probability Paul did not expect that any angel from heaven would descend to preach to the Galatians, and still less did he expect that any such messenger would proclaim the Judaizing message. He used this extravagant language to make the point that truth is superior to personality, and that the message which he was preaching should be inviolate no matter who proclaimed its opposite. Its truth was so unalterable that the very act of opposing it would merit a curse.

Explanation: Figures of Form

1. *Irony*

> *But it is good to be zealously sought in a good matter at all times, and not only when I am present with you.*
> (4:18)

The figure of irony appears only in the text quoted above, and in a very mild form. It relates to the Galatians' enthusiasm over Paul's first visit. Evidently they received him joyfully and treated him with honors. His physical weakness, which might naturally make him repulsive to them, did not prevent their listening to his message and accepting it. Upon his removal others had come in who had courted their interest so zealously that Paul was forgotten. He reminded them that they should be faithful in his absence as well as in his presence. The statement of the principle is an ironical reminder of what they had not done. The irony closely ap-

---

8. Gal. 1:8; 4:15; 5:12. See chart.

proaches sarcasm and innuendo; it is not the dramatic irony of the Greek tragedies.

2. Litotes

> *They zealously seek you in no good way.*
>
> (4:17)

Litotes is the affirmation of a truth by denying its opposite. Frequently it carries with it a sense of lowering the statement which a positive affirmation would make. To say that X "is not a bad man" is not quite so convincing as to say that he is a good man. When Paul described the Judaizers as zealously seeking the Galatians "in no good way," the implication was that the Judaizers were hypocritical, and that their real motives in cultivating the friendship of the Galatians were impure.

3. Meiosis

> *. . . against such there is no law.*
>
> (5:23)

Meiosis is understatement of a fact for the sake of effect, the opposite of hyperbole. The last clause of Galatians 5:23 is an understatement of the truth which Paul was seeking to emphasize. Had he said that the fruit of the Spirit was in accord with the law, or that it fulfilled the law, his statement would have been less forceful than this figure of speech has made it. How could there be a law against the qualities which are enumerated here: love, joy, peace, longsuffering, kindness, goodness, faithfulness, meekness, self-control? These cannot conflict with the requirements of God's law; on the contrary, they bring it to perfection.

4. Euphemism

> *I would that they that unsettle you would even go beyond circumcision.*
>
> (5:12)

Occasionally in the Pauline writings euphemism appears when some act or situation needs to be expressed in milder terms than its usual name. The English translation of Galatians 5:12 is a euphemism; for "go beyond circumcision" does not convey the brutal wish that is contained in the Greek text. The real meaning is that if the Judaizers propose to insist upon circumcision, they should mutilate themselves after the fashion of the pagan priests who did so as an act of worship, and that they would thus bring an end to their kind by depriving themselves of the power of reproduction. Some commentators have censured Paul for his harsh language and harsher sentiments.[9] Evidently he felt that those who insisted on legalistic ritualism as a means of salvation might just as well go all the way back to a fanatic heathenism. The language was intended to express extreme disgust rather than to perpetrate a coarse jest.

5. *Rhetorical Question*

> *For am I now seeking the favor of men, or of God? or am I striving to please men?*
>
> (1:10)

The use of rhetorical questions has already been discussed somewhat under the occurrence of figures in massed groups.[10] Such questions jolt the thinking of the reader by making him formulate a reply in his own mind. Paul knew perfectly well the answers to these inquiries, and asked them for effect rather than for information. The obvious answer to the questions quoted above is "No."

From the foregoing treatment of figures of speech one may see the extent to which the power of any argument is dependent upon them. They become the media through which the truth is pictured in the minds of men.

---

9. A. Lukyn Williams, *Galatians* in *Cambridge Greek Testament*, (Cambridge, University Press, 1914), p. 117.
10. *Supra*, pp. 138, 139.

THE TECHNIQUE OF TOPICAL STUDY

THE TOPICAL METHOD

CHAPTER VII

THE TECHNIQUE OF TOPICAL STUDY

The Topical Method

T HROUGHOUT each book of the Bible runs a web of topical structure, representing the leading ideas of the book's composer. Sometimes the topical themes are the main subject of the book; sometimes they are incidental to its discussion. No topics, however casually mentioned, are inconsequential in Bible study; for often that which is apparently incidental is really fundamental because it is taken for granted, and is a basic assumption in the thinking of the author.

The Nature of Topical Study

The topical method of study is valuable because it provides a means whereby one subject may be selected from the many subjects which are expressed or implied in a given book of the Bible, and may be studied separately in relation to its context. When such a topic is theological in nature, the topical study becomes mainly doctrinal and is treated as part of the theological approach; or when a person is the topic, the study is really biographical.

Two types of topical study are possible. The direct method, which is the easier, consists in the isolation of some word or phrase by the simple means of listing its verbal occurrences, as a concordance would list them in the order of their appearance in the text. The items of the list may be classified in accordance with their usage, and may be analyzed to provide a definition for the concept which they represent and to show its various meanings. The evaluation of the concept as a whole results from the integration of these usages and meanings with their application. The indirect method follows the same pattern, except that a general idea is traced instead of a fixed phrase. In the former case, one word usually embodies the topic; in the latter case, several words may be employed.

Since most topical studies are usually of the direct type, the sample given here is of that class. In order to avoid trivialities, research should be undertaken for its importance to the book of the Bible which is being studied, and for its pertinence to the practical needs of one's own day. Topical study includes, then, (1) the collection of all materials relevant to a given theme; (2) the definition of that theme by means of the data so collected; (3) the classification of usages of the term denoting the theme; (4) the relation of these usages to the context; and (5) the conclusions to be drawn from the foregoing process.

An Example of Topical Study

The Collection of Material

As an illustration of this kind of study the use of "law" in Galatians is presented.

SECTION	REFS	CONTEXT	SPECIAL USE (Greek phrase)
Introduction 1:1-9			
Biographical Argument 1:10-2:21	2:16 2:16 2:16 2:19 2:21	man is not justified by the works of the law that we might be justified ... not by the works of the law by the works of the law shall no flesh be justified I through the law died unto the law if righteousness is through the law, then Christ died for nought	*ex ergon nomou* *ex ergon nomou* *ex ergon nomou* *dia nomou, nomoi* *dia nomou*
Theological Argument 3:1-4:31	3:2 3:5 3:10 3:10 3:11 3:12 3:13 3:17 3:18 3:19 3:21 3:21 3:21 3:23 3:24 4:4 4:5 4:21 4:21	Received ye the Spirit by the works of the law? doeth he it by the works of the law? as many as are of the works of the law are under a curse in the book of the law that no man is justified by the law before God is evident the law is not of faith Christ redeemed us from the curse of the law A covenant confirmed by God the law ... doth not disannul If the inheritance is of the law ... What then is the law? Is the law then against the promises of God? If there had been a law given which could make alive ... righteousness would have been of the law we were kept in ward under law the law is become our tutor *to bring us* unto Christ born under the law that he might redeem them that were under the law ye that desire to be under the law do ye not hear the law?	*ex ergon nomou* *ex ergon nomou* *ex ergon nomou* *tou nomou* *en nomoi* *ho nomos* *tou nomou* *ho nomos* *ek nomou* *ho nomos* *ho nomos* *nomos ho dunamenos* *ek nomou* *hypo nomon* *ho nomos* *hypo nomon* *hypo nomon* *hypo nomon* *ton nomon*
Practical Argument 5:1-6:10	5:3 5:4 5:14 5:18 5:23 6:2	a debtor to do the whole law ye who would be justified by the law For the whole law is fulfilled in one word ... ye are not under the law . against such there is no law . . so fulfil the law of Christ	*ton nomon* *en nomoi* *ho nomos* *hypo nomon* *nomos* *ton nomon tou Christou*
Conclusion 6:11-18	6:13	For not even they who receive circumcision do themselves keep the law	*nomon*

The Definition of the Topic

The word "law" (Greek: *nomos*) is one of the most important terms in Galatians. It does not occur in the introduction, but in the three main sections of the book it appears thirty-one times, and once in the conclusion. Its use is most frequent in the theological argument where, of course, the topic is most significant.[1]

The meaning of the term is quite clearly defined in Galatians 3:17, where the law is identified with the Mosaic code of spiritual, moral, and ceremonial principles, given four hundred and thirty years after the time of Abraham. In 3:10 allusion is made to "the book of the law," which plainly refers to the Torah or Pentateuch. In those passages where the word *nomos* is accompanied by the definite article it refers to the Jewish law as written in the Old Testament.

The Classification of Usages

The word "law" is also used without the article in Galatians, chiefly in certain picked phrases which convey specialized meaning. The absence of the article usually means that the quality of the given concept is stressed rather than its identity, although in this context it refers to the Mosaic law as the chief embodiment of the concept.[2] "Law," then, in these instances, refers to the system of thought or the code of action involved rather than to any particular document. One of these usages is *ex ergon nomou*, translated into English "by the works of the law." Perhaps a more accurate rendering would be "by law-works." Six times this phrase appears,[3] and in three of the six occurrences it is used to assert that man is not justified by law-works; while in two of the remaining three instances it implies that neither the

1. For a full discussion, see Burton, *op. cit.*, pp. 443-460.
2. See Robertson, *op. cit.*, p. 796. "In general when *nomos* is anarthrous in Paul it refers to the Mosaic law. . ."
3. Galatians 2:16, (three times), 3:2, 3:5, 3:10.

receiving of the Spirit nor the working of miracles — both ot which were evidences of spiritual vitality in the Christian community — was a product of law-works. The sixth use of this phrase expresses origin rather than agency: "as many as are of law-works." Those who assume that they may be justified on legalistic grounds are by this phrase characterized as under the curse of the law, since they have not performed all that the law requires.

A similar phrase, *ek nomou,* translated "of the law," occurs twice in Galatians 3:18 and 21. Like *ex ergon nomou* it implies agency or source. Galatians 3:18 negates the possibility that the Christian's inheritance can be obtained by law. Galatians 3:21 denies that righteousness can be derived from law. Both exclude the law as a source of the Christian life.

A parallel expression, 'through the law" (Greek: *dia nomou*), occurs twice. The two expressions differ more in origin than in effect, since *dia nomou* implies agency by mediation. Twice it occurs in the text of Galatians: in 2:19, where Paul says, " I *through the law* died unto the law," and in 2:21, "if righteousness is *through the law,* then Christ died for naught." The former of these states a fact; the second states an hypothesis which is really contrary to fact. The one illustrates what the law has accomplished in putting the flesh to death; the second points out what the law failed to do. These two usages, plus the threefold statement that the law is not a source of justification, comprise the total discussion of the subject in the biographical section of Galatians. They announce the main theme of Galatians, and define the biographical and theological channels of argument.

The phrase "by the law" (Greek: *en nomoi*), or, more literally, *in law,* occurs twice, in 3:11 and 5:4. It refers not so much to means as to sphere of operation. "That no man is justified in the sphere of law before God is evident" might be a profitable translation of 3:11. The change of emphasis from source or agency to environment or sphere is indicated by the preposition *en.*[4] The believer in Christ is lifted to a wholly new plane of living. He works no longer within the restrictions of the law, but is emancipated from them.

The idea of subjection or limitation is conveyed by still another phrase, "under the law" (Greek: *hypo nomon*), which is used five times in the text.[5] The first of these defines its own use by the illustration attached to it. Being "under law" is compared to the status of a minor child who is virtually in a state of slavery until he can be owned publicly by his father as the heir of the family, and so be given a larger measure of adult liberty. It means, then, that one is circumscribed by law in order that he may ultimately be given the standing of a fuller sonship in Christ. The law fulfils the function of a guardian or of a preceptor who keeps the prospective heir from youthful indiscretions, and who trains him for the day when he shall be ready to enter upon his inheritance. The introduction to heirship is achieved through Christ, who himself was "under law" in order that He might by His redemption make us sons of God.

The Relation of the Topic to the Text

The relation of this aspect of law to the general structure of Galatians appears when the development of the topic is compared with the outline of the epistle. No allusion to the law occurs in the introduction, where Paul stressed the "gospel" which he preached. His presentation of truth was by preference positive rather than negative; and he desired that his argument might be a defense of justification by faith rather than an attack on legalism.

The Biographical Argument

The first six uses of the term "law" are in the last part of the biographical argument at the point where Paul terminated

---

4. For a good illustration of this usage elsewhere in Pauline writing, see Romans 2:12.

5. Galatians 3:23, 4:4, 4:5, 4:21, 5:18.

the account of his controversy with Peter at Antioch. These uses outline the significance given to the law in Galatians; for the first three (2:16) emphasize the futility of the law as a system of salvation by works; the fourth and fifth (2:19) state succinctly the relation of the believer to the law; and the last formulates in vigorous words the proposition that summarizes the whole argument of Galatians: "If righteousness is through the law, then Christ died for nought" (2:21). The conflict over law and grace is thus viewed from the theological, personal, and logical aspects. Theologically, salvation cannot be both by works and by grace; personally, release from the law must become real in the life of the believer; and logically, if the law can bestow complete holiness upon its observer, then the death of Christ is unnecessary.

The Theological Argument

The main development of this topic is interwoven with the theological argument of the book, and can scarcely be severed from it. Nevertheless, the two are not identical, and the interpretation of Paul's concept of law can be dealt with apart from textual procedure.

From 3:2 to 3:18 the law is shown to be of negative value in the development of Christian experience.

1. The observance of the law will not bring the promise of the Holy Spirit to one's personal life. (3:2)

2. The observance of the law is not the key to the constant miraculous power which God supplies. (3:5)

3. The attempt to fulfill the law only places man under a curse; for he must perform its requirements perfectly unless he wants to receive the judgment for failure. The law means perfection, or judgment. (3:10)

4. The law cannot restore man to a place of favor with God once he has sinned. (3:11)

5. The law cannot confer the inheritance of maturity which the justified man should possess. (3:18)

From this description of the impotence of the principle of law to redeem man from the guilt and slavery of his sin, the author turned to a discussion of the positive value of the law. "What then is the law?" he asked; and then hastened to answer his own question by saying that the law is a temporary expedient which was introduced to restrain human evil until the Seed should come unto whom the promise had been made (Gal. 3:19). It brought conviction upon men by its standard of holiness so that they felt their need of a savior (3:22), and so the law, by its standard of holiness and by its condemnatory admonitions, made men see their need of Christ (3:24). In due time the Seed came, and with His advent those who believed in Him were released from the law as a system, and were introduced to grace. Nowhere does Galatians say that under the new regime the moral standards of God are lowered, or that the law was a mere human convention to be discarded summarily. It is, rather, like an outworn garment of childhood which served a useful purpose, but which is no longer necessary to the mature man.

The Practical Argument

Having settled the relation of the law to Christian thinking, Paul turned in the practical argument of Galatians to discussing the relation of the law to the new life which the Christian receives through the Holy Spirit.

Paul's first affirmation was that the law must be completely abandoned as a means of achieving spiritual perfection. There can be no halfway house between works and grace. If the law be observed ceremonially with a view toward achieving a standing with God, then Christ is of no profit. By so doing one is obligated to perform all the law, and so to take a backward step (5:3, 4).

Secondly, the essence of the law may be retained through holding to its central means of fulfillment: "Thou shalt love thy neighbor as thyself." [6] Jesus Himself had quoted this passage as one of the two great commandments which summed up all the law and the prophets.[7] The law, then, is not to be discarded as an expression of the effects of holiness, but it can never be the true cause of holiness. The highest fulfillment can be produced only by the indwelling of the Holy Spirit, who brings forth fruitage in the life that the law cannot condemn (5:23), and an unselfish service for others that completes the requirements of the law of Christ. Perhaps the latter phrase refers to the law by which the Lord Jesus Christ lived, as He expressed it in the Sermon on the Mount (Matt. 5 to 7), which went further than the Mosaic law in the stringency of its ethical and spiritual demands.

Conclusion

The last reference to the topic of law in Galatians appears in 6:13, which is part of the conclusion. Paul's statement is like the parting shot in a duel, or like the last unanswerable rebuttal in a debate. "For not even they who receive circumcision do themselves keep the law; but they desire to have you circumcised, that they may glory in your flesh." He charged the legalists with inconsistency and malice: inconsistency in that they did not obey the law perfectly themselves; malice, because their main motive was not zeal for the law, but jealousy of others' freedom. Law is unable to produce the objective which it desires. The principle of the cross, not the principle of legalism, avails to justify men before God.

---

6. Lev. 19:18.
7. Matt. 22:34-40.

ANALYZING THE TEXT

The Analytical Method

CHAPTER VIII

ANALYZING THE TEXT

The Analytical Method

THE METHODS of study previously described have dealt with the book of Galatians as a whole. The broad sweep of this book and its significance have been kept in the foreground rather than minute study of any one segment of its text. Such an approach enables the student to grasp broadly the main theme and the subordinate topics contained in a given work, but does not afford to him a close understanding of the detailed statements and implications in it. In order to ascertain exactly what a given body of text says, one should employ the analytical method.

The analytical method consists of three distinct stages: the mechanical layout, which involves rewriting the text in a form that will reveal the grammatical structure; the formulation of an outline which will show by reasoning back from the grammatical structure to the meaning how the inner thoughts of the text are related to each other; and the recording of personal observations on the text as thus analyzed, in order to find both the explicit and implicit truths which it contains. All three procedures of this method are now applied to the practical argument in Galatians (5:1-6:10), which constitutes the third and final main division of the book.

Mechanical Layout

The practical argument begins after the transitional statement of Galatians 5:1: "For freedom did Christ set us free:

165

stand fast therefore, and be not entangled again in a yoke of bondage." In this first paragraph comprising verses 2 through 12, Paul reviewed the futility of circumcision and the logical antithesis between the freedom of Christ and the bondage of legalism from which the Galatians had been emancipated. In thus preparing for the continuation of the application of his teaching, Paul also defined the three personal elements in the situation by three pronouns: "you," "I," and "they." "You" referred to the Galatians, who had been freed by Christ, and who would henceforth think only in terms of freedom (10). "I" referred to Paul, who considered himself the champion of freedom and who defended his consistency (11). "They" were the people who upset the Galatians (12), upon whom Paul pronounced maledictions (12) and predicted that they would be judged (10). The first paragraph is therefore a resumé of the whole case with a brief statement of its practical implications which he intended to elaborate in the following paragraphs.

The part selected for analysis constitutes the bulk of this practical section, comprising paragraph 10 in the Greek text.[1] It contains the application of the principles of freedom for which the theological section has argued at length, and asserts what the result of the application of these principles will be.

The process of mechanical analysis consists of rewriting the given text in such form that the grammatical components of the paragraph are clearly discernible. The main statements of the paragraph, whether declarations, questions, or commands, are placed at the extreme left-hand margin of the sheet. Each line contains one main statement and its modifiers, provided that there is not more than one modifier in each class, and provided that the modifier is not of extraordinary length. Subordinate clauses and phrases are indented above or below the lines of the main statement, depending upon whether they precede or follow it in the order of the text. Thus in 6:1 the

---

1. *Supra*, p. 31

conditional clause, "even if a man be overtaken in any trespass," is indented above the line of the main statement, "restore such a one in the spirit of gentleness"; while "ye who are spiritual," which adds to "brethren" by defining still further the subject of the verb, is indented below the line, since it occurs in the middle of the verse. Two or more modifiers, including subordinate clauses or phrases or plural objects, are usually written directly beneath the word on which they depend, unless they are so brief that they can be retained conveniently in the original order of the text.

In making any analysis of this type, the paragraph is the unit for mechanical dissection. Chapter and verse divisions are ignored, except as they may be noted in the margin for reference in locating the lines of the text. All chapter and verse divisions are arbitrary, and not infrequently they are wrong. For instance, a better division than the break between chapters 5 and 6 would be between 5:24 and 5:25, where a new subject is introduced. Outlines should follow the thought as indicated by the grammar rather than by artificial or traditional arrangement.

Coordinate clauses connected by *and, but, either, or, neither, nor,* and *for* are generally regarded as containing main statements, and are written from the extreme left-hand margin. Sometimes the conjunction *for* is difficult to evaluate. It may simply introduce a statement fully coordinate with the one that precedes it, or it may make an explanation which seems quite secondary to the main line of thought. Such a usage occurs in verse 17, where the explanation of the mutual opposition of flesh and spirit is subordinate to the main command, "Walk by the Spirit." Furthermore, the second *for* clause in this section, "for these are contrary the one to the other," is so completely subordinate in thought as to be virtually parenthetical. In this instance, it may be treated as introducing a subordinate thought, and so may be listed as a modifier.

Lists of names, qualities, or actions are listed in vertical columns for the sake of clarity. Leaders (. . .) indicate that part of the text has been removed to another position because of its subordinate relation to the sentence as a whole.

Outline

The second stage after laying out the text mechanically in grammatical arrangement is the creation of an outline. An analytical outline should be textual; that is, it should follow the order and content of the text in its headings and subheadings. Textual outlines can be constructed most easily by ascertaining first the main paragraphs of the text, or the main topical sections, which will give the principal divisions of the outline. In each of these divisions the main declarative or imperative verbs will usually show what the next subheads ought to be; and modifiers will indicate what the smaller subpoints are.

In the text of Galatians 5:13 to 6:10 there are three main lines of thought. The first is contained in 5:13-15, in which Paul stated the proper and improper use of liberty. The second division, 5:16-24, beginning with the declarative, "But I say, Walk by the Spirit," defines the positive conduct of the free Christian through the contrast of the works of the flesh and the fruit of the Spirit. The outcome of this life in the Spirit is above law: "against such there is no law" (5:23). The third section contains the principles of the social application of liberty, and justifies the new freedom by the universality of its beneficial effects: "Let us work that which is good toward all men" (6:10). No comment is necessary on the details of the outline, which will speak for themselves.

Although the section to be analyzed is only a part of the third main division of Galatians, and is not therefore a completely independent unit, it will be treated as a separate unit for the purpose of demonstrating the technique of the analytical method. The headings of the following outline should be renumbered if they are to be integrated with the outline of the entire book as previously given.[2]

---

2. *Supra*, p. 35.

Analysis of Galatians 5:13 to 6:10

13 For ye, brethren, were called for freedom;
 only *use* not your freedom for an occasion to the flesh,
 but through love be servants one to another.
14 For the whole law is fulfilled in one word,
                    even in this:
                        Thou shalt love thy neighbor
                            as thyself.
15   if ye bite
                and devour   one another
 But . . . . . . take heed that ye be not consumed one of another.
16 But I say,
        Walk by the Spirit,
        and ye shall not fulfil the lust of the flesh.
17   For the flesh lusteth against the Spirit,
            and the Spirit   against the flesh;
            for these are contrary the one to the other;
                    that ye may not do the things that ye would.
        if ye are led by the Spirit,
18 But/. . . . . ye are not under the law.
19 Now the works of the flesh are manifest,
            which are *these*:
                        fornication,
                        uncleanness,
                        lasciviousness,
20   idolatry,
                        sorcery,
                        enmities,
                        strife,
                        jealousies,
                        wraths,
                        factions,
                        divisions,
                        parties,
21   envyings,
                        drunkenness,
                        revellings,
                        and such like;
        of which I forewarn you,
                even as I did forewarn you,
                that they who practise such things shall not inherit
                            the kingdom of God.
22 But the fruit of the Spirit is
                        love,
                        joy,
                        peace,
                        longsuffering,
                        kindness,
                        goodness,
                        faithfulness,

Outline of Galatians 5:13 to 6:10

THE LIFE OF LIBERTY 5:13-6:10

A. The Privilege of Liberty   5:13-15

  1. The Negative Restriction   13b
  2. The Positive Command   13c
  3. The Free Fulfillment of Law   14
  4. The Danger of Abuse of Freedom   15

B. The Individual Practice of Liberty in the Spirit   5:16-24

  1. Freedom from the Lusts of the Flesh   16
   (Parenthetical discussion of opposition
   of flesh and spirit)   17
  2. Freedom from the Law   18
  3. Contrast of Life in the Flesh and Life in the Spirit
   a. The works of the flesh

     (1) Nature: 19

       (a) Fornication
       (b) Uncleanness
       (c) Lasciviousness
       (d) Idolatry   20
       (e) Sorcery
       (f) Enmities
       (g) Strife
       (h) Jealousies
       (i) Wraths
       (j) Factions
       (k) Divisions
       (l) Parties
       (m) Envyings
       (n) Drunkenness
       (o) Revellings

     (2) Result: loss of the kingdom of God   21

   b. The fruit of the Spirit   22

    (1) Nature:

      (a) Love
      (b) Joy
      (c) Peace
      (d) Longsuffering
      (e) Kindness
      (f) Goodness
      (g) Faithfulness

Analysis of Galatians 5:13 to 6:10 — Continued

23   meekness,
                               self-control;
            against such there is no law.
24 And they that are of Christ Jesus have crucified the flesh
                               with the passions ⎫
                               and the lusts   ⎬ thereof.

25   If we live by the Spirit,
     By the Spirit let us also walk.

26 Let us not become vainglorious,
                       provoking one another,
                       envying one another.
6:1   even if a man be overtaken in any trespass,
     Brethren/. . . . . . . restore such a one
     ye who are spiritual, |in a spirit of gentleness;
                           |looking to thyself,
                                  lest thou also be tempted.

 2 Bear ye one another's burdens,
    and so fulfil the law of Christ.
 3   if a man thinketh himself to be something when he is nothing,
    For/. . . . . .he deceiveth himself.
 4 But let each man prove his own work,
    and then shall he have his glorying
                       |in regard of himself alone,
                       |and not of his neighbor.

 5 For each man shall bear his own burden.
 6 But let him that is taught in the word communicate
                            |unto him that teacheth
                            |in all good things.

 7 Be not deceived;
    God is not mocked;
    for whatsoever a man soweth
       that shall he also reap.
 8 For he that soweth . . . . shall . . . . . reap corruption;
        |unto his own flesh |of the flesh
    but he that soweth . . . . shall . . . . . reap eternal life.
         unto the Spirit |of the Spirit
 9 And let us not be weary in well-doing:
    for . . . . we shall reap.
                    |in due season
                    |if we faint not.
10.   as we have opportunity,
    So then,/. . . . . . . let us work that which is good
                       |toward all men,
                       |and especially toward them
                                        that are of the
                                        household of the
                                        faith.

Outline of Galatians 5:13 to 6:10 — Continued

Observations

Theory

The third stage in the analytical study of a text is observing the phenomena that appear in it. Mechanical analysis simply arranges the text so that its component parts are easily accessible; and the outline affords a clue to its organization. Observations deal with the individual points of interest which the student can find in the material that has been put before him. Such procedure is similar to preparing a dinner: mechanical analysis is like preparing the food for serving; the outline is like setting the table and arranging the courses; and the observations are like the portions which the diner selects as he fills his plate.

Observations, then, are the notations of significant items which can be used for instruction and for devotion. In order to be most effective as stimuli for thinking they should be classified so that they will not become collections of trite remarks or the endless reiteration of wearisome platitudes. The outline will often suggest some direction for detailed search in the text, or one may pursue the time-honored method of answering six questions, each of which begins with "W": (1) Who? (2) What? (3) When? (4) Where? (5) Why? (6) Wherefore?

Who? relates to the personalities mentioned in the text, whether they are discussed in characters, or introduced in dialogues, or assumed as the author or authors.

What? involves the action or content of the text, and sometimes includes also what is implied as well as what is actually recorded. Usually the outline will answer this question quite fully.

When? should list all the time clues in the context, whether they pertain to the action of the narrative or to the thought concerning it. For instance, the development of Paul's mission as described in Galatians 1 and 2 relates to the action of the narrative; the comment on that development belongs to the thought concerning it, and may pertain to quite a different time.

Where? deals with geographic locations, whether streets, or cities, or provinces. These should always be compared with diagrams or maps in order that the full meaning of the author's allusions may be made clear.

Why? probes the reason for the action or thought behind the item observed. The reader should always seek the cause for the action or utterance that is recorded, and also the reason for recording it. Interpretation is formulated reason, and is always dependent upon the answer to this question.

Wherefore?, the last question, cannot be answered from the text alone, since it concerns the interrelation of the results of the foregoing questions with the student himself. Since the Bible is the Word of God, its utterances have a distinct message for men, and all the truths found in it will have application to human experience at one time or another. The fuel for an intelligent devotional life must be drawn from the conclusions which each one makes for himself under the guidance of God's Spirit. Intellect and heart alike should participate in this effort. A non-intellectual approach to the Scriptures results in weak sentimentalism or in empty traditionalism, while a coldly formal treatment is deadening to the spiritual faculties of both the teacher and the pupil. Both light and heat are needed in Bible study.

Not all of these questions are equally applicable to any one body of text. All will apply fairly well to a running narrative like the story of Acts, in which personalities, action, conversation, times, and places are presented. In an essay, such as this section of Galatians, personalities are not prominent; ideas take the place of action and of conversation; times and locations may have no place at all.

In demonstrating the art of observation in an analyzed text, no attempt will be made to exhaust the possibilities of the passage under discussion. Sufficient samples of procedure and results will be given to show how the work is done; but much material will be left for the reader to discover for himself.

Procedure

Beginning with the question *Who?* the first set of observations deal with the personalities concerned in the text. Three individuals or groups are involved in the situation: the writer, denoted by "I," who is exhorting his readers; the recipients, addressed by differing titles, who are to profit by his counsel; and God, who is introduced as the governing power of all life. Apart from such inferences as may be drawn from his conversation as a whole, the writer appears in eleven references:

```
I say ..........................................5:16
I forewarn you ...............................21
I did forewarn you ..........................   ..........21
If we live by the Spirit ........................25
By the Spirit let us also walk ....................25
Let us not become vainglorious .................26
Let us not be weary ...........  ....   .........6:9
We shall reap .................................9
If we faint not ................................9
As we have opportunity ........................10
Let us work that which is good .................10
```

Three of these passages are a direct reference to the first person singular. The others, which use the first person plural, might be interpreted as representing all believers, or as more characteristic of Christians in general than as informative about the author. Nevertheless, since they are in the first person, they may be treated as relating to the author. All of them represent the trend of his thinking at this particular point.

The first of these, "I say," expresses the central thought of Paul's mind in the practical argument of the epistle. As such, it represents also the central conviction of his life. For him,

the walk in (or by) the Spirit was the true key to all success-
ful living.

The second and third references to the first person singular
reflect the maturity of his experience and the depth of his concern for the Galatians. He had foreseen the dangers into
which they had fallen, and had sought consistently to warn
them against the evils of the flesh.

The first three uses of the plural "pronoun" (25, 26) confirm the idea resident in the first instance noted above. Living
by the Spirit, and keeping step in the Spirit by refraining from
strife were the guides of personal Christian conduct for the
writer, and he hoped that they could be for his readers also.

The last five uses of the plural pronoun identify the writer
more closely with his readers in a common effort and in a common hope of reaping a reward. Paul did not preach at the
Galatians, even though they had exasperated him by their conduct. Since he had reached the conclusion of his argument, he
desired to take them with him, not to drive them from him.

The readers are designated in a number of ways:

Brethren 5:13, 6:1
Ye who are spiritual 6:1
He that is taught in the word 6:6
They that are of the household of the faith 6:10

Each of these epithets presupposes a spiritual relation among
the believers themselves and between them and Christ. "Brethren" implies that Paul placed the Galatians on an equality with
himself as sons of God, in accordance with the statement in 4:
5, "that we might receive the adoption of sons." Paul's address,
"ye who are spiritual," may be descriptive of a group within
the Galatian church upon whose loyalty and spiritual integrity
he could rely in any crisis. It may be that Paul used this
phrase as a stratagem to enlist the cooperation of the entire
church. If they flattered themselves on their spiritual prow-
ess, they could convince him of it by their willingness and

ability to restore those who had fallen into error. Those who are "taught in the word" are the members of the congregation as distinct from the teacher. "Word" [8] is used most frequently in Paul's earlier epistles to denote the substance of the Christian message. Furthermore, the term translated "taught" means "instructed by word of mouth," [4] and pictures a person who is listening to the teaching of another and memorizing it as it is spoken. The normal believer, then, was educated in the message of the gospel so that he could understand and appreciate it. The phrase, "of the household of the faith," emphasizes the solidarity of the entire group as united in a family relationship based on common belief in Christ and in God. The sum of these epithets affords a rounded picture of the nature and relationships of the believer.

God is mentioned directly only once in 6:7: "Be not deceived; God is not mocked." He is the personal power behind the inexorable law of sowing and reaping, and He cannot be defied with impunity. Believer and unbeliever alike must realize that they are ultimately responsible to Him, and that His laws always prevail. Whether they profit or lose by them depends upon their relationship to them; for these laws can work as infallibly for those who sow to the Spirit as they do against those who sow to the flesh.

What? can best be answered by the use of the imperatives which are the main verbs of this passage and which consequently give the principal line of thought contained in it. The outline accompanying the mechanical analysis will provide a formulation of general content, but a chart of the commands will illustrate the trends of the practical argument.

---

3. Greek: *logos.* For comparable uses elsewhere, see I Thess. 1:6, 8; 2:13; II Thess. 3:1; I Cor. 1:18; 15:2.
4. Greek: *katechoumenos,* the origin of the English term, *catechumen.*

COMMAND	REF.	PERSON
Use[5] not your freedom	5:13	2
Be servants one to another	13	2
Take heed that ye be not consumed	15	2
Walk by the Spirit	16	2
Let us also keep step by the Spirit[6]	25	1
Let us not become vainglorious	26	1
Restore such a one	6:1	2
Bear ye one another's burdens	2	2
Let each man prove his own work	4	3
Let him that is taught communicate	6	3
Be not deceived	7	2
Let us not be weary in well-doing	9	1
Let us work that which is good	10	1

The list contains all second and third person imperatives, plus those introduced by "let us," which are virtually imperatives in the first person,[7] making a total of thirteen. No distinctive classifications can be made on the basis of the difference of persons. All of these imperatives accord in spirit with a liberty which is expressed by humility. They are the opposites of license, self-aggrandizement, strife, disunity, boastfulness, censoriousness, insularity, smugness, parsimony, carelessness, and discouragement. They represent a constructive use of the freedom which is in Christ. The intermingled use of first, second, and third persons simply shows that the writer is including every viewpoint. Sometimes he speaks in the third person concerning a hypothetical case; sometimes he exhorts his readers directly; and sometimes he enthusiastically includes

---

5. The Greek text contains no finite verb, but the italicized English is a fair representation of the meaning.

6. Original translation.

7. Technically, these are hortatory subjunctives. Robertson, *op. cit.*, p. 943, says: "In the first person this use of the subjunctive held its own always in lieu of the imperative." J. H. Moulton, *A Grammar of New Testament Greek*, Vol. I, *Prolegomena* (Edinburgh: T. & T. Clark, 1906), p. 175, says that it is fair to speak of three persons in the imperative mood, since the hortatory subjunctive differs from the imperative only in that the speaker is included in the command.

himself. The use of these commands should disabuse anyone of the delusion that spiritual liberty is equivalent to the indulgence of personal whims. True spiritual life recognizes definite obligations. Liberty consists in freedom from legalistic and moral restraint in order that one may do spontaneously what is right.

Some other phenomena in the text which are not directly connected with the outline are worthy of special note.

Differences in words similarly translated are important. An excellent illustration is the use of the word "walk" as applied to the Spirit in 5:16. "Walk by the Spirit, and ye shall not fulfil the lust of the flesh" [8] refers to the physical act of walking, and it is used figuratively of general personal conduct. In 5:25, "by the Spirit let us also walk," [9] a different verb is used which means "to keep step." Both verbs refer to Christian behavior, but the second is more definitely a word of social relationships, since it involves the concept of walking in rank with others, or in accordance with some rule that is common to all. The distinction is apt; for the former "walk" is applied to the contrast between the flesh and the spirit in the individual life, whereas the latter introduces a paragraph which discusses the social responsibilities of the Christian toward fellow-believers.

A second pair of words in this context deserves particular notice, since they are frequently posed as a "contradiction" in the Bible. In Galatians 6:2 is the statement, "Bear ye one another's burdens, and so fulfil the law of Christ." Verse 5 says, "Each man shall bear his own burden." A careful examination of the words behind the translation "burden" will resolve the difficulty. The "burden" of verse 2 is the Greek word *baros*, which means "a heavy weight," a crushing load which will overwhelm a man unless he is given assistance. The

---

8. Greek: *peripateite.* See Rom. 6:4; Phil. 3:17, 8.
9. Greek: *stoichomen.* Cf. Acts 21:24; Rom. 4:12; Phil. 3:16.

second "burden" is *phortion,* which usually refers to the normal load which an animal could carry, or to the cargo of a ship.[10] There is no essential conflict between these two texts which say that Christians should seek to relieve each other of excessive burdens, but that they should expect to carry their normal load of responsibilities.

Contrasts are sometimes directly introduced in order to illuminate the meaning of a truth. Compare the teaching on *spirit* and *flesh*:

SPIRIT	FLESH
Walk by the Spirit 5:16	Fulfil lusts of the flesh ..5:16
	Under the law (where
Led by the Spirit 18	flesh must be) 18
Fruit of the Spirit 22, 23	Works of the flesh 19-21
Sow to the Spirit 6:8	Sow to the flesh 6:8
Reap life 8	Reap corruption 8

These verbal contrasts are capable of expansion by viewing them in the light of their context. "Walking by the Spirit" implies an atmosphere of freedom in which the individual is prompted from within by the Holy Spirit, who is regarded as a friend and counsellor. "Fulfil the lusts of the flesh" depicts a slave who is driven by a tyrant's lash to carry out his orders. "Led by the Spirit" refers to an inner control; "under the law," to an outward compulsion. Much the same idea prevails in the next contrast; for "fruit" is the product of natural growth, whereas "works" are the result of toilsome effort. "Life" and "corruption" are self-explanatory. Through these antitheses Paul set forth the advantages of the life of liberty in the Spirit in contrast to the life of bondage in the flesh.

The definitions of these two terms, "spirit" and "flesh," vary with their usage. "Spirit" in the writings of Paul may

---

10. For the uses of *baros* elsewhere in the writings of Paul, see I Thess. 2:6, where it is translated "burdensome." *Phortion* is the word used by Jesus in Matt. 11:30, "my burden is light", and in Acts 27:10, referring to the cargo of the ship. Moulton & Milligan, *op. cit.,* p. 674, quote papyri which use the word in the same sense.

refer to a component element of man's being (I Thess. 5:23), or to the Holy Spirit as a distinct personality (Eph. 4:30), or to the realm of living in which a Christian should abide (Rom. 8:9), or to a particular attitude or disposition (I Cor. 4:21). The majority of his uses of the term, however, apply to the Holy Spirit, whom he usually prefers to call the Spirit of God. In Galatians, out of eight cases of "spirit" with the definite article, seven refer directly to the personal Spirit of God. Receiving the Spirit (3:2) is a definite crisis in spiritual experience which involves the entrance of an outside power or personality into human life. The Spirit is given directly by God (3:5) in fulfillment of His promise (3:14). In Galatians 4:4-6 Paul stated that God sent forth both His Son and the Spirit of His Son. The two are distinguished from each other and are distinct individuals with differing functions. In Galatians 5:17, "spirit" and "flesh" could easily be understood as denoting only separate aspects of man's moral nature. The definite article indicates that the reference to spirit is to be interpreted as the Holy Spirit, who holds the flesh in check and restrains it from its full expression. The same personal spirit is intended in 5:22, where the article recurs, and where a similar contrast is implied between the works of the flesh and the fruit of the Spirit.

In one or two instances in Galatians the word "spirit" does not apply to the Holy Spirit at all. In 6:1 the phrase "in a spirit of gentleness" is synonymous with an "attitude of gentleness." In 6:18, it refers to the human spirit.

"Flesh," [11] another of Paul's favorite words, occurs in Galatians eighteen times. Two of these, by metonymy, refer to humanity in general as "flesh and blood," or "no flesh" (1:16; 2:16). Three passages relate to the physical body (4:13, 14;

---

11. Greek: *sarx*. For a full discussion of these two terms, see Burton, *op. cit.*, pp. 486-495.

6:12). One uses the phrase "in (the) flesh" as a synonym for the present life in the physical realm (2:20). The others signify the moral nature of man apart from God and uncontrolled by the Holy Spirit, with the possible exception of 4:23, where the phrase "after the flesh" [12] may mean the basis of natural or physical birth. Apparently Paul made this word the name for the force or tendency in man's nature which gravitates away from God toward sin. There is no indication that Paul identified "the flesh" solely with the body. The "works of the flesh" listed in 5:19-21 are not simply the deeds of the body, but are the expression of a corrupt nature which are contrasted with the natural production of the Spirit of God. Unlike many of the philosophers of his day, he did not believe that matter was inherently evil, nor that victory over evil could be achieved by asceticism.

In no less than four passages (4:29; 5:16, 19-22; 6:8) the Spirit and the flesh are purposely contrasted. Both enter into the believer's experience; but the true believer who has the faith of the Son of God (2:20) cannot live by the flesh. He sows to the Spirit, from whom he reaps life and peace.

Another point of interpretation should be noted in Galatians 5:17. The verse reads: "For the flesh lusteth against the Spirit, and the Spirit against the flesh; for these are contrary the one to the other; that ye may not do the things that ye would." The last clause is ambiguous. Does it mean that the power of the Spirit over the flesh exists for the purpose of keeping us from doing the evil that we might otherwise practice? Or does it mean that because of the conflict we are incapable of attaining to the full realization of our spiritual ambitions? Robertson and Lightfoot both regard it as a result clause,[13] which means that the inner conflict of flesh and spirit

---

12. Greek: *kata sarka*. For a similar usage elsewhere, in which the moral aspect has no place, see Rom. 1:3.
13. Robertson, *op. cit.*, p. 998.
   Lightfoot, *op. cit.*, p. 210.

keeps man from perfection under the law. Paul's dilemma in Romans 7:19, "For the good which I would I do not; but the evil which I would not, that I practise," is an expression of this principle. On the other hand, Burton contends that this clause is a purpose clause which applies to both flesh and spirit, "in the sense that the flesh opposes the Spirit that men may not do what they will in accordance with the mind of the Spirit, and the Spirit opposes the flesh that they may not do what they will after the flesh." [14] The former interpretation is preferable, since the text seems to emphasize the outcome of the conflict rather than its indeterminate character. The succeeding verse shows that the Spirit's power is directed not only to restraint of evil, but to victory over it; and that in the leadership of the Spirit there is an answer to the life which is frustrated by the flesh.

When? and *Where?* do not enter into the analysis of this part of Galatians, for the discussion is psychological rather than historical. For observations illustrating these two points, better examples may be found in the discussions of chapters 1 and 2.

Why? should this particular section of Galatians have been written? Two reasons are patent. First of all, it completed the argument of the epistle by showing that the inner problems of man could not be solved by legalism. Circumcision of the flesh could have no direct effect upon unholiness of spirit; and if man is trusting in the outward ceremony, the reality of Christ would do nothing for him. Fulfillment of the law as God gave it could come only from a spontaneous love for God and for one's neighbor, which is the creation of the Holy Spirit. From Him emanate all the graces that are the fruit of perfection.

Second, the practical application of the principle afforded an opportunity for the instruction of the Galatian churches with reference to their peculiar needs. The imperatives mentioned

---

14. Burton, *op. cit.,* p. 302.

above were really a series of exhortations. The epistle was designed not only for correcting theoretical errors, but also for inculcating a deeper Christian character in the Galatians.

Wherefore? What conclusion may be drawn from the foregoing analysis? The principle of spiritual liberty becomes the heritage of every believer in Christ. The consequences of the teaching of Galatians 5:13 to 6:10 affect all his thinking. They confront every Christian with the alternative of two atmospheres in which he may live, legalism or liberty. They inform him that he must inevitably be dominated by one of two forces, the spirit or the flesh. They define the outcome of two lives, sowing to the flesh, which brings corruption, and sowing to the Spirit, which brings life. They characterize the Christian as one who has "crucified the flesh with the passions and the lusts thereof" (5:24).

The personal conclusions to be drawn from this teaching may be tabulated as follows:

1. Liberty in the Spirit is available to any Christian.

2. Liberty is obligatory upon every Christian if he is to fulfil the purpose of his redemption.

3. Liberty for the Christian is the opposite of fleshly indulgence.

4. Liberty means the full development of personality through the graces which result from the control of the Spirit.

5. Liberty produces a fruitful and spontaneous life.

INTERPRETING SCRIPTURE BY SCRIPTURE

THE COMPARATIVE METHOD

CHAPTER IX

INTERPRETING SCRIPTURE BY SCRIPTURE

The Comparative Method

Although the meaning of Galatians must have been intelligible to its first readers even if they were unacquainted with any of the other books that are included in the Biblical canon, its value to the modern student can be greatly enhanced when it is studied in conjunction with the rest of Scripture. No one book of the Bible can be interpreted adequately without comparing it with all the others, in order that its relation to them may be seen and that its allusions to them may be explained. This use of one passage of Scripture to illustrate or to interpret another because of some similarity or contrast inherent in both of them is called the comparative method.

The basis of this method is threefold. It depends upon the relation of a given passage to other passages in the works of the same author. Any writer who has a well defined set of beliefs or concepts will repeat them or refer to them in all of his productions. If they form the foundations of his thinking, he will inevitably build his main teachings upon them. Galatians is a basic part of the corpus of Paul's letters, because it contains the very heart of the Pauline gospel. One should expect, therefore, that its teaching will be supplemented or duplicated by other epistles written by the same author. Cognate passages in Paul's other letters may state even more clearly than Galatians the truth of which it speaks, and will thus act as commentaries upon its contents.

A second basis of the comparative method is the relation which obtains between the Old and New Testaments. The

New Testament is related to the Old Testament as the fruits of a tree are related to its roots. Without the roots the fruits cannot be explained, for they depend upon the roots for their origin and sustenance. Without the fruits the roots are futile, for the tree could not fulfil its purpose without them. The roots of divine revelation are to be found in the Old Testament, where the beginnings of the knowledge of God, the experience of sin, and the promise of redemption may be found. The fruits of that revelation are in the New Testament, where Christ is revealed. Without Him the Old Testament is a story without an ending, a path that leads nowhere. The New Testament teaching can often best be explained by showing its parallel in some Old Testament source, while a comparison of the Hebrew shadow with the Christian substance will often make a seemingly unimportant incident of history glow with new value.

The third basic principle of this method is the broadest and the most cogent. Scripture is a unit. If its ultimate author is the Holy Spirit (I Pet. 1:10-12), the student has a right to expect that there will be a deep unity holding together all parts of the written revelation. Despite the fact that they were written by authors of differing nationality, tastes, occupations, characters, and purposes, and at widely separated places and times, there is a common subject that draws them to a focus: namely, Christ. If one part depends upon another part for its source material, a comparison of the two should show the relationship between them and should make the unity clearer.

The Use of the Method

The initial step in the comparative method is the establishment of some common point of similarity between the passages to be compared. Most often it hinges upon some topic such as a doctrine or an event which is discussed in two or more kindred passages. It may be a person whose activities or character illustrate God's method of dealing with men or who has made a spiritual contribution to knowledge. Quite frequently an Old Testament passage is quoted in the New Testament without giving any discussion of its context. In such a case a comparative study of the original source of the quotation together with its application by the New Testament author broadens and deepens its meaning.

The Comparative Study of a Topic

The comparison of two passages containing a similar topic may be illustrated by the parallel consideration of Galatians 3:5-14 and Romans 3:31-4:16. Both have the common theme of law and faith; both refer to the Old Testament as a source; and both deal with the revelation of God to Abraham. Furthermore, both are written by Paul, so that they constitute two varying approaches to the same doctrine by the same author. They should, therefore, supplement each other, and the presentation in Romans should help to explain the content of Galatians.

The argument of the passage in Galatians is theological and personal. Abraham is introduced as a single illustration of the principle that the blessings of God come by faith rather than by law. Just as God attributed righteousness to Abraham because of his faith, so those who exercise a similar faith are considered to be Abraham's children, and consequently are fit recipients of the blessing of Abraham, which Galatians equates with the promise of the Spirit (3:14). The entire paragraph, including the argument from the Old Testament texts, is the answer to the initial question propounded in Galatians 3:5: "He that supplieth to you the Spirit . . . . *doeth he it* by the works of the law, or by the hearing of faith?"

The teaching of Romans 3:31-4:16 begins at the same point of law and faith (3:31). The same key text, "Abraham believed God, and it was reckoned unto him for righteousness" (Gen. 15:6) is quoted, and the entire paragraph stresses the importance of faith. Its emphasis is different from that of the

A COMPARISON OF TOPIC IN
GALATIANS 3:5-14 and ROMANS 3:31-4:16

	TEXT OF GALATIANS		TEXT OF ROMANS
3:5	He therefore that supplieth to you the Spirit, and worketh miracles among you, *doeth he it* by the works of the law, or	3:31	Do we then make the law of none effect through faith? God forbid: nay, we establish the law.
6	by the hearing of faith? Even as Abraham believed God, and it was reckoned unto him for righteousness.	4:1	What then shall we say that Abraham, our forefather, hath found according to
		2	the flesh? For if Abraham was justified by works, he hath whereof to glory;
		3	but not toward God. For what saith the scripture? And Abraham believed God, and it was reckoned unto him for right-
7	Know therefore that they that are of	4	eousness. Now to him that worketh, the
8	faith, the same are sons of Abraham. And the scripture, foreseeing that God	5	reward is not reckoned as of grace, but as of debt. But to him that worketh not,
	would justify the Gentiles by faith, preached the gospel beforehand unto Abraham, *saying*, In thee shall all the		but believeth on him that justifieth the ungodly, his faith is reckoned for right-
9	nations be blessed. So then they that are of faith are blessed with the faithful Abraham.	6	eousness. Even as David also pronounceth blessing upon the man, unto whom God reckoneth righteousness apart
		7	from works, *saying*, Blessed are they whose iniquities are forgiven, And whose sins are covered.
		8	Blessed is the man to whom the Lord will not reckon sin.
		9	Is this blessing then pronounced upon the circumcision, or upon the uncircumcision also? for we say, To Abraham his faith was reckoned for righteousness.
10	For as many as are of the works of the law are under a curse: for it is written, Cursed is every one who con-	10	How then was it reckoned? when he was in circumcision, or in uncircum-
	tinueth not in all things that are written in the book of the law, to do them. Now	11	cision? Not in circumcision, but in uncircumcision: and he received the sign of circumcision, a seal of the righteous-
11	that no man is justified by the law before God, is evident: for, The righteous		ness of the faith which he had while he was in uncircumcision: that he might be
12	shall live by faith; and the law is not of faith: but, He that doeth them shall		the father of all them that believe, though they be in uncircumcision, that
13	live in them. Christ redeemed us from the curse of the law, having become a		righteousness might be reckoned unto them; and the father of circumcision
14	curse for us; for it is written, Cursed is every one that hangeth on a tree: that	12	to them who not only are of the circumcision, but who also walk in the steps of
	upon the Gentiles might come the blessing of Abraham in Christ Jesus; that		that faith of our father Abraham which
	we might receive the promise of the Spirit through faith.	13	he had in uncircumcision. For not through the law was the promise to Abraham or to his seed that he should
		14	be heir of the world, but through the righteousness of faith. For if they that are of the law are heirs, faith is made
		15	void, and the promise is made of none effect: for the law worketh wrath; but where there is no law, neither is there
		16	transgression. For this cause *it is* of faith, that *it may be* according to grace; to the end that the promise may be sure to all the seed; not to that only which is of the law, but to that also which is of the faith of Abraham, who is the father of us all.

kindred passage in Galatians, for its initial question is: "Do we then make the law of none effect through faith?" (Rom. 3:31) In Galatians, Paul is endeavoring to show the effect of faith upon the validity of the law.

The approach of Romans to this problem is therefore quite different. Its logic is as follows:

> If a man works for a goal, receiving his pay is not grace, but the payment of what he had earned.
> If a man acts on faith, he receives not what he has earned, but what the donor gives freely without regard to merit.
> The blessings of God are not given as a reward of labor, but as a free gift to those who exercise faith.
> In the case of Abraham, the status of righteousness was accorded to him before he had entered into the covenant of circumcision.
> Circumcision is therefore a recognition of a status already established, and not a means of acquiring it.
> The faith of Abraham, and not the circumcision, brought the blessing of God.
> Abraham, therefore, is the model for all, Jews and Gentiles alike, who wish to receive God's blessing.
> The final corollary is that if the inheritance comes through the law, then faith and the promise are both nullified.

Parallel in these two lines of argument are (1) the point of departure in the relations of law and faith, (2) the Old Testament example of Abraham, (3) the key passage of Genesis 15:6, which provides the basis of reasoning, (4) the idea that the blessing of God comes in response to faith, (5) the concept that those who exercise faith are "children" of Abraham (Gal. 3:7, Rom. 4:11, 16). Romans provides a broader theological foundation for the concept of salvation by faith, and shows that the heirship cannot be claimed through the law. The teaching of Galatians on the Holy Spirit is not given at this point in Romans, but is developed in the eighth chapter where it parallels Galatians 5:16-25.

The Comparative Study of a Character

The biographical method involves the collation of all data relevant to the characters of the book which is being studied, but a comparison of two specific events or passages can be classed under the comparative method.

The allusion to Titus (2:3) is brief, and contains little that describes him or that reveals why his name is mentioned in connection with the content of Galatians. He was a companion of Paul and Barnabas when they went up to Jerusalem for the interview with the leaders of the church there. He was a Greek who had not been brought up under Jewish law, and was therefore not circumcised, and he was not compelled to be circumcised by vote of the council. Evidently Paul mentioned him because he was an important witness to the broad stand taken by the leaders of the church before the Jerusalem Council. The language is a bit ambiguous; for when it says that Titus was not "compelled to be circumcised" (2:3), one might conclude either that Titus had successfully withstood the pressure of the Judaizers or else that he had submitted voluntarily. The former seems to be the more likely alternative, since Paul says of the Judaizers in this connection that they did not yield to them, "no, not for an hour" (2:5). "We" implies that Titus and Paul stood together, and that they made no material concessions whatsoever.

The comparison of this account with the other passages where Titus is mentioned serves to bring his personality into sharper relief. Next in chronological order of the books in which he is mentioned is II Corinthians, written from Macedonia to Corinth about the year 56. Acts is completely silent about Titus, but II Corinthians makes plain that he had accompanied Paul on the third journey, and that he had become one of Paul's most trusted lieutenants. If he joined Paul at Antioch (Acts 18:22, 23) he must have shared in the Galatian campaign, and have participated in Paul's long and effective ministry in Ephesus. Before Paul left Ephesus to enter

Macedonia Titus was despatched to Corinth to straighten out the tangled affairs of the church there. Upon leaving Ephesus, Paul proceeded to Troas, where he anxiously awaited Titus with some news of events in Achaia. Titus, however, did not appear (II Cor. 2:13), and Paul went on to Macedonia, hoping to meet him there. Paul's confidence in Titus and his affection for him are evident in the epithet which he applies to him, "Titus, my brother." Although Titus could not have been much older in Christian experience than Timothy, who was Paul's associate at this time and co-author of II Corinthians, it is noticeable that Paul calls Timothy "my son" (I Cor. 4:17). Titus was already a man of mature spiritual judgment, quite capable of handling the administrative problems which the rebellious and turbulent church at Corinth had created.

Titus probably had some misgivings about the result of his deputational visit to Corinth. Paul said that "his spirit hath been refreshed by you all" (II Cor. 7:13), as if he had anticipated more difficulties than he actually encountered. Paul had told him that the Corinthians would doubtless make things right, and he was relieved that Titus found his prediction true (II Cor. 7:14).

Titus' success in this difficult errand corroborates the impression given by the incidental reference in Galatians that he was a strong determined character. He refused to submit to the Judaizers at Antioch; he was not dismayed by the opposition at Corinth. Paul calls him a "partner and fellow-worker" (II Cor. 8:23), and endorses him thoroughly.

The next appearance of Titus in the canonical record is in the book that bears his name, written probably in the early sixties. By that time he was in Crete, where his ministry seems to have been much the same as it had been in Corinth (Titus 1:5). The Cretan church was in a deplorable condition, and needed desperately a strong hand to correct its evils and to bring order out of chaos. The advice which Paul gave in no way militates against the essential confidence which he had in

Titus as an executive. Paul expected that he would fulfil the task speedily and effectively, and gave instructions for rejoining him at Nicopolis (3:12).

The last allusion to Titus occurs in Paul's farewell letter to Timothy (II Tim. 4:10). He had gone to Dalmatia, but the object of his errand is not stated. Judging by the fact that a general dispersal of Paul's associates is chronicled in this passage, one might fairly conclude that Titus was one of a number who went in different directions to carry on an evangelistic ministry and to decentralize the group of leaders who were in danger of arrest by the Roman authorities. Paul himself wrote from Rome, presumably, where he was a prisoner (1:16, 17) after having been suddenly arrested somewhere during travels along the west coast of Asia Minor, possibly at Troas (II Tim. 4:20, 13). Titus had become an independent worker, launching out on his own mission to a territory where he had not previously worked with Paul.

The comparative study of allusions to Titus brings him partially out of the shadows in which time has obscured him. The qualities of bold leadership which made him the voluntary witness and aid to Paul and Barnabas as they championed the freedom of the Gentiles from the law made him an effective worker through the two decades that elapsed between his conversion at Antioch and the dispersion of the Pauline party at the time of Paul's death. He was a convincing demonstration of the validity of salvation for the Gentiles apart from the law. His ministry ranks with that of Timothy, who, though half Gentile, was circumcised because he was also half Jew (Acts 16:1-3), in order that no needless offense might be given to the Jewish brethren.

The Comparative Study of Old Testament Text

The comparative study of the New Testament use of quotations with their Old Testament setting affords two distinct benefits: a broader comprehension of the underlying thought of the text in which the quotations occur, and a better understanding of the interpretative method which the author employed. For purposes of comparison the same piece of text will be used here that appeared in the former diagram, with the Old Testament original in parallel columns, giving the English translation both of the Hebrew Massoretic text (ARV) and of the Septuagint.[1] Paul, as a Greek-speaking Jew of the Dispersion, used the Septuagint for general purposes of quotation, though doubtless he was acquainted with the Hebrew text as well.

In this short segment of Galatians are six quotations from the Old Testament, three of which are introduced by a formula of definite reference to the Old Testament (Gal. 3:8, 10, 13), and the remaining three are plainly cited by Paul with full knowledge of their origin. They are used as the basis for his argument for the priority of promise over law, and should therefore be selected to carry more weight than if they were merely illustrative.

The first point of comparison affects accuracy of quotation. Exact verbal accord between the quotations in Galatians and the original Hebrew text is difficult to establish, inasmuch as the Greek text of Galatians would have to be a translation in any case. On the basis of both the English and the Greek text the differences between Paul's quotations and his sources are relatively slight. His use of the LXX is demonstrated by Deuteronomy 27:26 and 21:23 which show a closer verbal resemblance between Galatians and the LXX than between Galatians and the Massoretic text. The remaining quotations, while not exact in every respect, are indeterminate in their relationship.

---

1. The American Standard Version is quoted as an accurate translation of the Massoretic Hebrew text, and the Bagster translation of the Septuagint is used for the LXX, after careful comparison with the originals. Deviations from the current translations or comments will be incorporated in notes.

A COMPARISON OF OLD TESTAMENT QUOTATIONS
WITH TEXT OF GALATIANS 3:5-14

NEW TESTAMENT		OLD TESTAMENT (Massoretic Text) (A. R. V. — 1901)	OLD TESTAMENT (SEPTUAGINT) (BAGSTER)
3:5 He therefore that supplieth to you the Spirit and worketh miracles among you, *doeth he it* by the works of the law, or by the hearing of faith?			
6 Even as Abraham believed God, and it was reckoned unto him for righteousness.	Gen. 15:6	And he believed in Jehovah; and he reckoned it to him for righteousness.	And Abram believed God, and it was counted to him for righteousness.
7 Know therefore that they that are of faith, the same are sons of Abraham.			
8 And the scripture, foreseeing that God would justify the Gentiles by faith, preached the gospel beforehand unto Abraham, *saying*, In thee shall all the nations be blessed.	Gen. 12:3	In thee shall all the families of the earth be blessed.	In thee shall all the tribes of the earth be blessed.
9 So then they that are of faith are blessed with the faithful Abraham.			
10 For as many as are of the works of the law are under a curse: for it is written, Cursed is every one who continueth not in all things that are written in the book of the law, to do them.	Deut. 27:26	Cursed be he that confirmeth not the words of this law to do them.	Cursed *is* every man that continues not in all the words of this law to do them.
11 Now that no man is justified by the law before God, is evident: for, The righteous shall live by faith:	Hab. 2:4	Behold, his soul is puffed up, it is not upright in him; but the righteous shall live by his faith. (In his faithfulness. ARV mg.)	If he should draw back, my soul has no pleasure in him: but the just shall live by my faith.
12 and the law is not of faith; but, He that doeth them shall live in them.	Lev. 18:5	Ye shall therefore keep my statutes, and mine ordinances; which if a man do, he shall live in them: I am Jehovah.	So shall ye keep all my ordinances, and all my judgments, and do them; which if a man do, he shall live in them: I *am* the Lord your God.
13 Christ redeemed us from the curse of the law, having become a curse for us: for it is written, Cursed is every one that hangeth on a tree:	Deut. 21:23	He that is hanged is accursed of God (the curse of God. ARV mg.)	For every one that is hanged on a tree is cursed of God.
14 that upon the Gentiles might come the blessing of Abraham in Christ Jesus; that we might receive the promise of the Spirit through faith.			

Although there are minor differences between the quotations and their original sources, the verbal disparities are not so great as to make the sources unidentifiable, nor even great enough to alter the sense materially. Paul has quoted the Old Testament faithfully in preserving the original meaning.

The second point of comparison relates to the correspondence between the thought or argument of Galatians and the underlying thought behind the context of the quotation. Taking the six quotations in series, a brief résumé will be given of the context of each and its bearing upon Galatians.

Even as Abraham believed God, and it was reckoned unto him for righteousness.

Genesis 15:6 is Abraham's reaction to one of the most important promises that God gave to him. At his call from Ur of the Chaldees, God had affirmed that through his descendants all families of the earth should receive a blessing (Gen. 12:3). The nature of this blessing was not defined at that time, and the means of its fulfilment was not apparent because Abraham had no children. For a number of years Abraham remained childless, and when God appeared again to him, Abraham suggested that perhaps the promise might be fulfilled by the formal adoption of his oldest servant, who would then become his acknowledged heir. Abraham and Sarah were too old to have children, and he knew it. God's reply affirmed that there would be a son born to him and Sarah. The prediction seemed impossible, but Abraham, accepting God's word despite all impossibilities, "believed God." This act of faith which appropriated what God had promised, and which threw into the hands of God the whole unseen future of his life, was accepted as righteousness by God. Not because of what he had done, but because he believed God against all external appearance he was placed in a new standing and was given the assurance of the continuance of divine favor.

The principle of accepting as fact what God promises and of acting on that promise is the basis of our salvation, or of justification before God.　Paul is using the text to establish the truth that God saves man not because of what man has, but because of what God can do for him.

The second passage, Genesis 12:3, is not quite so patent in its application.　The equation between justification by faith and the blessing promised through Abraham's seed is not categorically stated by the Old Testament.　The equation between the two may, however, be reached by the somewhat circuitous route of showing that the divine blessing of the nations must be spiritual.　What did God want to confer upon them that could come only through Abraham's seed?　The definition of this blessing will have to be traced through the historical prophecies and through the words of Jesus Himself, who was the seed of Abraham (Matt. 1:1) — a process longer than can be included here.　Paul's point, however, is valid that God's promise to Abraham included the Gentiles, and that His dealings with Abraham and his descendants were intended to be the preparation for a universal outpouring of salvation.

The next quotation from Deuteronomy 27:26 is part of the summary of the law which was to be chanted antiphonally by groups on Mts. Gerizim and Ebal after the people had crossed the Jordan and had entered Canaan.　These words, "Cursed be he that confirmeth not the words of this law to do them" indicate that the slightest failure to keep the law will bring down upon the violator the curse of God.　The legalist thus lives under the threat of a curse; for he can never be sure when he may disobey God's law.　He is constantly under the negative pressure of apprehension and fear, and his future is uncertain at best.　Legalism thus becomes pessimism; for the law can evoke only a negative righteousness, and its usual function is to condemn the guilty and not to produce a positive cure for evil.

On the other hand, the positive principle of faith is declared in Habakkuk 2:4, which Paul now weaves into the argument: ". . . the righteous shall live by his faith."　The immediate context in Habakkuk is not an abstract discussion of the merits of faith versus works as a means of salvation, but is a very concrete situation created by a political danger. Babylon had suddenly become a great military power, and was threatening the independence of all the small kingdoms of the Middle East. An invasion seemed imminent, and the prophet knew well that Judah would not have the force to resist it. Babylon would ride over their little kingdom like a steamroller over an ant-hill. The problem for Habakkuk, however, was not purely political. How could a just God, whom his nation had professed to worship, allow this godless heathen power to obliterate the righteous people whom He had chosen? Invasion was politically inevitable and morally inexplicable. The problem struck at the very root of the prophetic faith.

Wisely Habakkuk decided to wait and to listen for what God might communicate to him. God did speak, and gave the assurance that the righteous should live by his faith. Safety lay in trusting God, who could hold the enemy in check and who could rescue His people in spite of overwhelming odds. The principle of faith in God is the key to the moral dilemmas of life.

In the final chapter of his prophecy Habakkuk says:

Thou wentest forth for the salvation of thy people,
For the salvation of thine anointed;
Thou woundedst the head out of the house of the wicked man,
Laying bare the foundation even unto the neck.

Jehovah, the Lord, is my strength;
And he maketh my feet like hinds' feet,
And will make me to walk upon my high places.

Faith begets confidence, and the prophet's dismal forebodings are transformed into triumphant song by the assurance that God is greater than evil — great enough to save His people.

Paul takes the same principle and shows how the individual may apply it to the particular dilemma of the justice and mercy of God in dealing with the individual. If God's justice condemns the sinner who breaks the law, and if God's mercy would save him, let him cast himself upon God and see what provision God will make.

The solution of this dilemma does not lie in the law itself. Leviticus 18:5 says:

> *Ye shall therefore keep my statutes and mine ordinances; which, if a man do, he shall live in them.*

The genius of the law is action rather than faith. Keeping it is properly a consequence of righteousness, not a cause of it. Salvation by faith and salvation by works are mutually exclusive. The statement in Leviticus is part of a general direction which God gave to Israel in anticipation of their entering Canaan, and, like Deuteronomy 27:26, is declarative of a broad principle, not just of a specific precept. But if, as the passage from Deuteronomy says, man under the law is living under the threat of God's curse, how can faith take him out from under it? Law itself is powerless. What provision has God made for the sinner?

The last question of the paragraph provides the final answer. Paul says: "Christ redeemed us from the curse of the law, having become a curse for us; for it is written, Cursed is every one that hangeth on a tree." The source in Deuteronomy 21: 22, 23 is part of an incidental regulation pertaining to executions:

> *And if a man have committed a sin worthy of death and he be put to death, and thou hang him on a tree; his body shall not remain all night upon the tree, but thou shalt surely bury him the same day; for he that is hanged is accursed of God.*

Christ, who had not broken the law, by His hanging on the cross came under the curse, and so He took the sinner's place. The Seed of Abraham, the heir of promise, has assumed the penalty of a broken law so that the blessings available through Him might come freely upon the Gentiles.

From the principles enunciated in these six quotations, and illuminated by their context Paul builds part of his theological argument. The comparative method shows how the ideas of the Old Testament, whether contained in statements of fundamental principles or in apparently incidental regulations, fit together in the presentation of the gospel of which the Old Testament was the forerunner.

The exegetical method of Paul was probably learned from the rabbinical school in which he had been trained. It is surprising that he did not indulge in more wholesale "spiritualization" than is found in his epistles. He could and did use an allegory upon occasion, as Galatians 4:21-31 shows, but he seldom did so. His interpretation may at times have been indirect, but as the text shows he was able to extract the central principle from verses of Scripture and to apply it to the problems of his own day.

The application of the comparative method to any passage of Scripture in the foregoing fashion will usually enable the reader to understand better both its historical and intellectual background, and to enter into the mind of the author who penned it. It will tie different parts of the Bible together, and will make increasingly real the unity of revelation which has its focus in the person of Christ.

FROM LETTER TO SPIRIT

THE DEVOTIONAL METHOD

CHAPTER X

FROM LETTER TO SPIRIT

The Devotional Method

THE VARIOUS types of study which have been applied to Galatians all have their place in a well-rounded approach to the book; but no one of them, nor all of them together will produce the effect for which the book was originally designed. Neither Paul nor the Spirit who prompted him may have anticipated that all of the readers of Galatians would possess keen critical acumen or would be versed in the method of mechanical analysis. These methods may produce a good understanding of the letter of the epistle; but a mere knowledge of its facts and style will never impress its real message upon a believing heart. The crown of all study is the devotional method, by which the truths ascertained through the various means already described are integrated and applied to the needs of the individual.

Definition

Although the devotional method is always improved by the use of these other methods, it need not be dependent upon them. It can be used by itself, and may be applied to a single verse or phrase as well as to the book as a whole. It is of greatest value, however, when used in conjunction with the others, and when it pervades them. Devotional study is not so much a technique as a spirit. It is the spirit of eagerness which seeks the mind of God; it is the spirit of humility which listens readily to the voice of God; it is the spirit of adventure which pursues earnestly the will of God; it is the spirit of adoration which rests in the presence of God. The obvious purpose of this epistle was not to prepare the Galatians for passing an examination, but to prepare them for living a life.

The object of devotional study is to find a center around which thought and conduct may be integrated in terms of holiness and service. Since the Scriptures are the message of God, their teaching by precept and by example will provide that center, and its applicability will be determined by its analogy with the existing situation.

Integration

Three centers for devotional study are always possible, and are applicable to almost every text or body of text:

1. What does the passage teach about Christ?
2. What new truth does it afford?
3. How does it illumine personal experience?

In applying these three criteria to the last section of Galatians (6:11-18), one should observe that this portion of the epistle is intended to be a summary of the meaning of the whole book. Paul gave the parting thrust and the final testimony that brought his teaching out of the realm of abstract argument into that of concrete personal reality. He felt what he debated; the liberties for which he had fought so valiantly were a vital part of his own experience.

In this summary he emphasized Christ in relation to the cross. The motives of the Judaizers were not, he said, a true zeal for the law, but an unwillingness to be persecuted for the cross of Christ (6:12). They were not ready to face the shame which it brought to them as followers of the One who had died under the curse of the law. They asked to retain the favor of those who had rejected Christ and at the same time to remain Christians. In order to maintain this inconsistent position they relied upon the weight of numbers, and so insisted that all others should join them in their strict adherence to the ceremonial law.

The cross of Christ, when used as a test for measuring the attitude of the inner man, discloses ulterior motives and shows men to be what they really are. In comparison with the death of Christ how much religious zeal proves to be only selfish ambition! How much righteousness is really prompted by the fear of being caught in doing wrong! How much profession is sheer hypocrisy! As the cross revealed the selfishness and malice in the Judaizers, so it reveals the sins and shortcomings of all others.

The cross, however, is not an intolerable burden nor an end to all joy. Paul boasted that through it he had found liberty. By representative union with Christ in death the believer finds that the world is crucified unto him and he unto the world. As surely as Christ has died, and so has severed the connection between the world and Himself, so surely the believer is emancipated from the claims of the world upon him. Its ideals are no longer acceptable because he has taken Christ's ideals for his own; its fashions are seen to be temporal, and the things of God, eternal. He, too, has been cut off from the world by the cross and is no longer reckoned as part of it. He has been placed in an entirely new environment which can only be described as a new creation (6:15).

For this reason liberty is mastery by Christ. "I bear branded on my body the marks of Jesus" (6:17) is a piece of imagery taken from slavery. A slave was often marked with the brand of his master, or was described by some distinguishing scar to show to whom he belonged. Paul, thinking possibly of the scars left by stonings and stripes, spoke of the marks that indicated that he belonged to Christ. As the cross had left scars on Christ, so had Paul's sufferings for Christ left scars on him. These visible mementos of persecution and struggle he wore gladly, even proudly. Unlike circumcision, they were the result of the voluntary choice of his mature years, incurred not because of custom but because of love. Paradoxically enough they were the signs of Paul's freedom, for as the servant of Christ he was emancipated from custom and ceremony and was independent of Pharisee and prelate alike. Christ is more than circumcision, and salvation is more than legalism.

From these observations springs the second corollary that "neither is circumcision anything, nor uncircumcision, but a new creature" (6:15). Neither observance of circumcision nor abstinence from it is consequential; the real issue lies in whether or not one possesses the new life which makes him a new creature in Christ. If he does possess it, nothing else matters; if he does not possess it, no external rites can impart it. Self-effort cannot produce spiritual vitality. It must begin by the impartation of the Holy Spirit who masters the individual and brings him under the standard and sway of the cross.

The conclusion of the book, then, provides the model for personal experience. It began with a crisis. "Crucified," as Paul used the term, must refer to some definitive experience in space and time which worked in his life the miracle of transformation. Having passed that crisis, he lived in a new realm from which old things had passed away and in which all things had become new. The rule of the new realm was conformity to Christ. The positive emphasis insured regularity of conduct and peace of heart. There was neither license nor bondage in the ideal Christian experience, but a poised loyalty to Christ that produced a happy obedience. Self-denial and suffering may have necessarily accompanied it, but they were regarded not as obstacles to be overcome nor as meritorious works, but as the incidental price which must be paid for the natural development of the Christian life. The final prayer of Galatians is that the grace of Christ might be with the spirit of the brethren in daily circumstance.

Expression

The expression of Christian devotion cannot be reduced to any set formula, neither can a fixed pattern be devised whereby any individual may profit from a devotional study of the

Scriptures. No one text will be equally illuminating or stimulating to all its readers in the same way, and the benefit of one's study will vary with his circumstances, his temperament, and his spiritual maturity. In Paul's case devotion was expressed in his urgency, for he wrote the epistle in his own hand because of the intensity of his apprehension for the safety of his followers. It was revealed in his intellectual exertion as he thought his way through the problems that confronted him and the Galatians. It was proved by his endurance of physical hardships which left the marks on his body to which he referred. It produced an indifference to all attractions and pleasures that might divert his attention from Christ. It was manifested in the patience and peace of his spirit, as he commended the grace of Christ to his recalcitrant churches. Perhaps the acme of Paul's devotional life as reflected in Galatians can best be summarized in the famous hymn of Isaac Watts:

> *When I survey the wondrous cross*
> *On which the Prince of glory died,*
> *My richest gain I count but loss,*
> *And pour contempt on all my pride.*
>
> *His dying crimson, like a robe,*
> *Spreads o'er his body on the tree;*
> *Then am I dead to all the globe,*
> *And all the globe is dead to me.*
>
> *Were the whole realm of nature mine,*
> *That were a present far too small;*
> *Love so amazing, so divine,*
> *Demands my soul, my life, my all.*

BIBLIOGRAPHY

Askwith, E. H. *The Epistle to the Galatians: An Essay on Its Destination and Date.* London: Macmillan and Co., 1902. Pp. xx, 153.

Bacon, Benjamin W. *Introduction to the New Testament.* New York: The Macmillan Co., 1924. Pp. xv, 285.

——————— *Commentary on the Epistle of St. Paul to the Galatians,* in *The Bible for Home and School.* New York: The Macmillan Co., 1909. Pp. vii, 135.

Barnett, Albert Edward *Paul Becomes A Literary Influence.* Chicago: University of Chicago Press, 1941. Pp. xiii, 277.

Beet, J. Agar *A Commentary on St. Paul's Epistle to the Galatians.* Fifth Edition. London: Hodder & Stoughton, 1885. Pp. xxiv, 232.

Burton, Ernest D. *A Critical and Exegetical Commentary on the Epistle to the Galatians.* In series of the *International Critical Commentary.* New York: Charles Scribner's Sons, 1920. Pp. lxxxix, 541.

Calvin, John *Commentaries on the Epistles of Paul to the Galatians and Ephesians.* Grand Rapids, Michigan: Wm. B. Eerdmans Publishing Co., 1948. Pp. x, 383.

Chafer, Lewis S. *Systematic Theology.* Eight volumes. Dallas, Texas: Dallas Seminary Press, 1948.

Chase, F. H. "The Galatia of the Acts: A Criticism of Professor Ramsay's Theory," *Expositor,* Series IV, Vol. VIII, pp. 401-419. London: Hodder & Stoughton, 1893.

Colwell, E. C. "Biblical Criticism: Lower and Higher," *Journal of Biblical Literature,* LXVII (1948), 1-12.

Conybeare, W. J., and Howson, J. S. *The Life and Epistles of St. Paul.* New Edition. Grand Rapids, Michigan: Wm. B. Eerdmans Publishing Co., 1949. Pp. xxii, 850.

Davidson, Samuel *An Introduction to the Study of the New Testament.* Second Edition Revised and Improved. Two Volumes. London: Longmans, Green, & Co., 1882.

Davis, J. D. "Galatians," in *A Dictionary of the Bible.* Philadelphia: Westminster Press, 1924. Pp. 242, 243.

Dods, Marcus "Galatians" in Hastings' *Dictionary of the Bible.* New York: Charles Scribner's Sons, 1900. Vol. I, 91-98.

Duncan, George S. *The Epistle of Paul to the Galatians.* New York: Harper & Bros., Publishers, [1934], Pp. xxi, 199.

Ellicott, Charles J. *A Commentary, Critical and Grammatical, on St. Paul's Epistle to the Galatians.* Andover, Mass.: W. J. Draper, 1860. Pp. 183.

Emmet, Cyril W. *St. Paul's Epistle to the Galatians.* New York: Funk & Wagnalls, 1916. Pp. xxxi, 68.

Erdman, Charles R. *The Epistle of St. Paul to the Galatians.* Philadelphia: Westminster Press, 1930.

Farrar, F. W. *Messages of the Books of the Bible.* Two volumes. London: Macmillan & Co., Ltd., 1909.

————————"The Rhetoric of St. Paul," *Expositor,* Series I, X (1879), 1-27.

Findlay, George G. "Galatians" in *International Standard Bible Encyclopaedia.* Grand Rapids, Michigan: Wm. B. Eerdmans Publishing Co. Vol. II, 1155-1163.

————————*The Epistle to the Galatians. The Expositor's Bible.* Grand Rapids, Michigan: Wm. B. Eerdmans Publishing Co. Pp. 461.

Godet, F. *Introduction to the New Testament. Particular Introduction, I. The Epistles of St. Paul.* Translated from the French by William Affleck. Edinburgh: T. & T. Clark, 1894. Pp. xiii, 621. See Pp. 181-237.

Goodwin, Frank J. *A Harmony of the Life of St. Paul.* New York: American Tract Society, 1895. Pp. 240.

Govett, Robert *Govett on Galatians.* London: Thynne, 1930. Pp. 266.

Hayes, Doremus A. *Paul and His Epistles.* New York: The Methodist Book Concern, 1915. Pp. 508.

Hogg, C. F. and Vine, W. E. *The Epistle of Paul the Apostle to the Galatians, with Notes Exegetical and Expository.* London: Pickering & Inglis, (1922).

Hovey, Alvah *Commentary on the Epistle to the Galatians,* in *American Commentary on the New Testament.* Philadelphia: American Baptist Publishing Society, 1890. Pp. 78.

Howson, J. S. *The Metaphors of St. Paul* and *The Companions of St. Paul.* Boston: American Tract Society, 1873. Pp. 91, 211.

Ironside, Henry A. *Expository Messages on the Epistle to the Galatians.* New York: Loizeaux Bros., 1940. Pp. 235.

Julicher, Adolf *An Introduction to the New Testament.* London: Smith, Elder, and Co., 1904. Pp. 68-78.

Knox, D. B. "The Date of the Epistle to the Galatians," *The Evangelical Quarterly,* XIII (1941), 262-268.

Knox, Wilfred L. *The Acts of the Apostles.* Cambridge: University Press, 1948 Pp. viii, 121.

Lake, Kirsopp *The Earlier Epistles of St. Paul.* London: Rivingtons, 1911. Pp. 253-316.

———————— and Lake, Silva *An Introduction to the New Testament.* First Edition. New York: Harper & Bros., Publishers, 1937. Pp 124-130.

———————— "Simon, Cephas, Peter," *Harvard Theological Review,* XIV (1921), 95-97.

LaPiana, George "Cephas and Peter in the Epistle to the Galatians," *Harvard Theological Review,* XIV (1921), 187-193.

Lightfoot, J. B. *Saint Paul's Epistle to the Galatians.* London: Macmillan & Co., Ltd., 1921. Pp. 384.

Luther, Martin *Commentary on Galatians.* A New Edition corrected and revised by Erasmus Middleton. Grand Rapids, Michigan: Wm. B. Eerdmans Publishing Co., 1930. Pp. 536.

Macgregor, James *The Epistle of Paul to the Churches of Galatia.* Edinburgh: T. & T. Clark, 1879, Pp. 127.

Machen, J. Gresham *The Origin of Paul's Religion.* Grand Rapids, Michigan: Wm. B. Eerdmans Publishing Co., 1947. Pp. 329.

Marsh, F. S. "Galatians," in Hastings' *Dictionary of the Apostolic Church.* New York: Charles Scribner's Sons, 1916. I, 430-437.

Meyer, Heinrich *Critical and Exegetical Handbook to the Epistle to the Galatians,* New York: Funk & Wagnalls Co. 1884. Pp. 275.

Moffatt, James *An Introduction to the Literature of the New Testament* New York: Charles Scribner's Sons, 1911. Pp. xli, 630.

Moulton, J. H. *A Grammar of New Testament Greek,* Volume I, *Prolegomena.* Edinburgh: T. & T. Clark, 1906. Pp. xx, 274.

Moulton, J. H. and Milligan, G. *The Vocabulary of the Greek New Testament.* Grand Rapids, Michigan: Wm. B. Eerdmans Publishing Co., 1949. Pp. xxxii, 705.

NOVUM TESTAMENTUM GRAECE cum apparatu critico curavit D Eberhard Nestle, novis curis elaboravit D. Erwin Nestle. Editio vicesima prima, Stuttgart: Priviligierte Wurttemburgische Bibelanstalt, 1952.

Ramsay, Sir William "Galatia," in Hastings' *Dictionary of the Bible.* New York: Charles Scribner's Sons, 1900. Vol. II, 81-91.

——————— *The Church in the Roman Empire Before A. D. 170.* New York: G. P. Putnam's Sons, 1893 Pp. 97-111.

——————— "Galatia," in *International Standard Bible Encyclopaedia* Grand Rapids, Michigan: Wm. B. Eerdmans Publishing Co. Vol. II. 1154, 1155.

———————*A Historical Commentary on St. Paul's Epistle to the Galatians.* New York: G. P. Putnam's Sons, 1900. Pp. xi, 477.

Rendall, Frederic "Galatians" in *Expositor's Greek Testament.* Vol. IV. Grand Rapids Michigan: Wm. B. Eerdmans Publishing Co. Pp. 120-200

——————— "The Galatians of St. Paul and the Date of the Epistle," *Expositor,* Series IV, Vol. IX. London: Hodder and Stoughton, 1894 Pp. 254-264.

Ridderbos, Herman N. *The Epistle of Paul to the Churches of Galatia.* Translated by H. Zylstra from the Dutch. In *The New International Commentary on the New Testament,* Grand Rapids, Michigan: Wm. B. Eerdmans Co., 1953, pp. 238.

Roberts, A. and Donaldson, J., *The Ante-Nicene Fathers,* 10 Vols. Grand Rapids, Mich.: Wm. B. Eerdmans Co., 1950-51.

Robertson, A. T. *A Grammar of the Greek New Testament in the Light of Historical Research.* Third Edition. New York: George H. Doran Co., 1919.

Ropes, James H. *The Singular Problem of the Epistle to the Galatians.* Cambridge, Mass.: Harvard University Press, 1929. Pp. 46.

Round, Douglas *The Date of St. Paul's Epistle to the Galatians.* Cambridge: University Press, 1906. Pp. vi, 72.

Schmiedel, P. W. "Galatians," in *Encyclopaedia Biblica.* London: Adam & Charles Black, n. d. Vol. II, 1589-1618.

Scott, E. F. *The Literature of the New Testament.* New York: Columbia University Press, 1932. Pp. 145-153.

Smith, David *The Life and Letters of St. Paul.* New York: George H. Doran Company, n. d. Pp. 193-221.

———— *Our Lord's Earthly Life.* New York: George H. Doran Company, n. d.

Stamm, R. T. and Blackwelder, O. F. "Introduction and Exegesis" and "Exposition of Galatians" in *The Interpreter's Bible,* Vol. X. New York: Abingdon-Cokesbury Press, 1953. See pages 427-593. Written from liberal standpoint.

Strahan, James "Galatians," in Hastings' *Dictionary of the Apostolic Church.* New York: Charles Scribner's Sons, 1916. Vol. I, 427-430.

Tenney, Merrill C. *John: The Gospel of Belief.* Grand Rapids, Michigan: Wm. B. Eerdmans Publishing Co., 1953. Pp. 321.

THE SEPTUAGINT VERSION of the Old Testament, with an English Translation. London: S. Bagster and Sons, Ltd. New York: James Pott & Co., 1896.

Thiessen, Henry C. *Introduction to the New Testament.* Fourth Edition. Grand Rapids, Michigan: Wm. B. Eerdmans Publishing Co., 1948.

Toy, Crawford Howell *Quotations in the New Testament.* New York: Charles Scribner's Sons, 1884. See pp. 190-193.

Trench, Richard C. *Synonyms of the New Testament.* Tenth Edition, corrected and improved. Grand Rapids, Michigan: Wm. B. Eerdmans Publishing Co., 1948.

Turner, C. H. "Chronology," in Hastings' *Dictionary of the Bible.* New York: Charles Scribner's Sons, 1900 Vol. I, 424.

Watkins, C. H. *St. Paul's Fight for Galatia.* Boston: The Pilgrim Press, 1914. Pp. 312.

Williams, A. Lukyn *The Epistle of St. Paul the Apostle to the Galatians,* in *Cambridge Greek Testament.* Cambridge: The University Press, 1914. Pp. xlix, 160.

Wood, C. T. *The Life, Letters and Religion of St. Paul.* Edinburgh, T. & T. Clark, 1925. Pp. 64-91, 92-97.

Wood, William S. *Studies in St. Paul's Epistle to the Galatians.* London: Rivingtons, 1887. Pp. xi, 163.

Wuest, Kenneth S. *Galatians in the Greek New Testament.* Grand Rapids, Michigan: Wm. B. Eerdmans Publishing Co., 1944. Pp. 192.

Zahn, Theodor *Introduction to the New Testament.* Translated from the Third German Edition by J. M. Trout, W. A. Mather, L. Hodous, E. S. Worcester, W. H. Worrell, R. B. Dodge, under the direction and supervision of M. W. Jacobus. Three volumes. New York: Charles Scribner's Sons, 1909.